INTRODUCTION

By Sidney L. Matthew

FOR SOME unknown reason this book has been a well-known secret for over half a century. Bobby Jones's biographer and constant companion, O.B. "Pop" Keeler (who accompanied Jones on 150,000 miles of adventures culminating in the "Impregnable Quadrilateral" known to generations as "The Grand Slam") penned it. Keeler got a good head start writing Jones's biography when *Down The Fairway* was published in 1927. But the story in that book stopped with Bob's capture of "The Double"—both U.S. and British Open Championships in the same year—1926. After Jones completed the cycle in the historic Grand Slam year of 1930, Keeler had to cobble together the rest of the story. He did this with the aid and assistance of his weekly news columns written about Jones for the *Atlanta Journal* and assorted other periodicals including the *American Golfer*.

Pop Keeler was especially suited to be the Boswell of Bobby Jones. He was a dyed-in-the-wool newspaperman with a nose for a good story and a "tar bucket mind." That's because everything that went into his mind stuck. There is even the true story of the occasion when Keeler reported on the final verdict of a court case. The day after the ruling, the judge lost his order. No problem. He simply dispatched his clerk to purchase a copy of Keeler's account in the newspaper and entered Keeler's version as the Court's official order. Within a day or two, the original order was discovered under a stack of papers and compared to the Keeler version. They were identical even to the punctuation marks!

INTRODUCTION

While Keeler was an astute observer of historical events with a keen eye for detail, it's clear that he didn't give Bob Jones the worst of his commentaries. Even so, there wasn't much negative to report anyway. The fact is that Jones didn't have any dust to sweep under the editorial carpet or skeletons in his closet. Jones was every bit the true American hero who was the same sterling character after five o'clock that he was during the championships. Keeler didn't have to fake his reporting of Jones's accomplishments because Jones didn't fake it. Supreme Court Justice Harry Blackmun gave one of the Jones lectures on ethics at Emory University in 1972 and commented on that one aspect of Jones's life that had previously gone unmentioned. "It is, it seems to me, the complete absence so far as I know or have read, of any besmirching or demeaning or unethical aspect in his legal or extra-legal career." Jones was, in a word, impeccable.

This account only covers Jones's life up to the age of 28 when he retired on top of the world of sport. It is undoubtedly the most triumphant journey ever traveled by any sportsman. Jones was simply better in his sport during this time than any other sportsman had ever performed in another sport. He is clearly the only one with the confidence and wisdom to retire on top of his game. Muhammed Ali, George Foreman, Michael Jordan, to name a few, haven't been able to do that.

Keeler's story of Jones's boyhood experiences is as charming as it is historic. He divides up Jones's career into the seven lean years and seven fat ones. Keeler suffers through each defeat as if he were the vanquished. And he revels in each triumph as if he were the one being cheered by adoring crowds throughout the world.

In this volume, you have perhaps the most magnificent combination as has ever existed in sport. What a boy's life!

Tallahassee, Florida, January, 2002

The Boys' Life of
BOBBY JONES

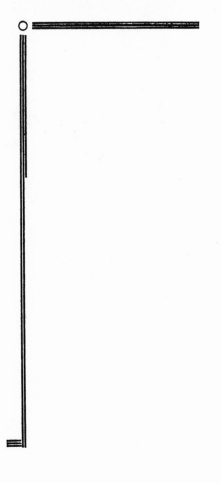

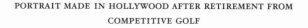

PORTRAIT MADE IN HOLLYWOOD AFTER RETIREMENT FROM
COMPETITIVE GOLF

The Boys' Life of
BOBBY JONES

by

O. B. KEELER

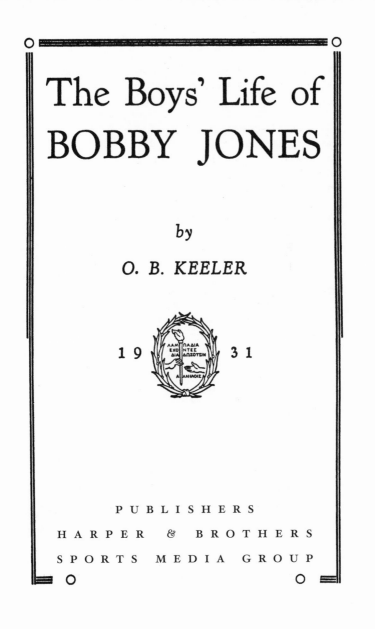

1 9   3 1

PUBLISHERS

HARPER & BROTHERS

SPORTS MEDIA GROUP

All inquiries should be addressed to:
Sports Media Group
An imprint of Ann Arbor Media Group LLC
2500 S. State Street
Ann Arbor, MI 48104

Printed and bound at Edwards Brothers, Inc., Ann Arbor,
Michigan, USA

08   07   06   05   04   1   2   3   4   5

Library of Congress Cataloging in Publication data on file.
ISBN 1-58726-100-6

THE BOYS' LIFE OF BOBBY JONES

Copyright, 1931, by Harper & Brothers

CONTENTS

ILLUSTRATIONS

ILLUSTRATIONS

FOREWORD

NOVEMBER 19, 1930, two days after Bobby Jones announced his retirement forever from competitive golf, there appeared on the stately editorial page of the London *Times* the following, under the heading, "Hail and Farewell":

"Having finished the work assigned to me," said George Washington to Congress, "I retire from the great theater of action." Today, some hundred and fifty years later, another American, in his own sphere almost equally famous, Mr. Bobby Jones, has taken leave of his public life; and the golfers of the world he has conquered may reply with the President of 1784, "Sir, you retire with the blessings of your fellow-citizens." Every single golfer who knows Mr. Jones, and thousands who have only watched him or even gazed upon his photograph, will hear of his decision with regret; but there will be few that do not, however reluctantly, acknowledge its wisdom. . . .

As a player of games he has done all that mortal man could do, and more than any man has done before. There is no championship of the first importance that he has not won, and this year he has set the coping-stone on his achievements by winning all four of them in one summer. Ever since as a boy of fourteen he played in his first

national championship a fierce light has been beating on
him, and he may well long to play the game that he loves
merely for fun. However much a man may love a game
for its own sake, to play it as Mr. Jones has done for
fourteen years is the hardest of work. It would exact a
heavy toll of any man, and no player that ever lived has
taken his game more to heart than he. By strength of
character he has subdued a naturally fiery temper till he
plays the game outwardly as a man of ice; but the flames
still leap up within. This has been one of the causes of his
success; no one of more phlegmatic or easy-going nature,
granted the same skill, could have achieved so much; the
greatest poetry will beat the best prose. But a player of
such a temperament, in everyday language, takes it out
of himself prodigally, and anyone who saw Mr. Jones
after his last round at Hoylake this summer must have
realized that the time was coming to call a halt.

The qualities that Mr. Jones has shown in his playing
life must needs serve him well in his working one. "I
have always been of opinion," said Mrs. Micawber, "that
Mr. Micawber possesses what I have heard my papa call,
when I lived at home, the judicial mind, and I hope Mr.
Micawber is now entering on a field where that mind
will develop itself and take a commanding station."

All British golfers will echo the words of that devoted
wife, and, while wishing Mr. Jones all good fortune in the
Law Courts, may yet hope that he will never desert us.
We cannot believe that he will. He is a member of the
Royal and Ancient Golf Club; he loves the breezes of
Fife as if he had been bred among them, and they will be
calling and calling in his ears to come back. For us he
can never come too soon and never too often.

It was of this editorial a few days later that the Prince of Wales, speaking at the Thanksgiving dinner of the American Society in London, said:

"Bobby Jones has attained what very few people in this country have done, and that is an editorial in one of our most sedate and respected journals."

And the Prince, with whom Bobby had often played golf, added:

"Not only does the great golfing community of Great Britain, but the whole of the sporting community, admire to the utmost his unique achievement, which I predict will never be beaten—namely, that of winning in one year, or ever winning, the four biggest golf trophies in the world. And we admire particularly the most graceful way in which he has retired."

When Bobby came home from the golfing wars, to find the rest that is so "pleasant after toil beneath a stranger sun," the *Atlanta Journal* said, editorially:

St. Andrews, Hoylake, Interlachen, Merion, and all his other shining fields—of these what more can be said than that we "have eyes to wonder, but lack tongues to praise." Yet, above the golfer's unexampled conquests, we see today the victories of the man. When purpose masters impulse, when patience rules hot blood and tingling nerves, when courage crowns itself with wisdom, when triumph clothes itself with modesty, and good sense is mated to good will, then is established the fairest of kingdoms and the happiest pages written in human history. Our master of golf is master of himself; therein lies his topmost trophy. He has done more than perform a feat. He has achieved a character, so that the world, while marveling at his game, pays highest tribute to his soul.

From endless columns and reams of editorials these excerpts serve as well as any to illustrate a perhaps surprising fact—that in attaining the position, not only of the foremost golfer of his era, but also of the foremost competitive athlete of the age, Bobby Jones has captured something in the admiration and the love of the two great English-speaking nations in no wise accounted for by his thirteen major championships in golf, or by the unparalleled season of 1930, when, by winning in succession all the four major titles of Great Britain and the United States, he entrenched his record safely and forever within what Mr. George Trevor of the *New York Sun* has called the "impregnable quadrilateral of golf."

"He has done more than perform a feat," says the *Atlanta Journal.* "He has achieved a character."

Perhaps in this little book I can tell you something of that, along with Bobby's career in golf. I saw much of his game. I attended twenty-seven major, or national, championships with him and numberless lesser events. I traveled with him 120,000 miles. And I am the only person in the world who saw him win all thirteen of his major titles.

I saw much of Bobby's game, in the fifteen years of his national and international career. I saw much of Bobby, too. And I know why they wrote those editorials, when, as the *New York Times* concluded:

> With dignity he quit the memorable scene on which he nothing common did or mean.

Perhaps I can tell you something of the boy who became the finest golfer in the world—and a finer boy than that.

O. B. K.

The Boys' Life of
BOBBY JONES

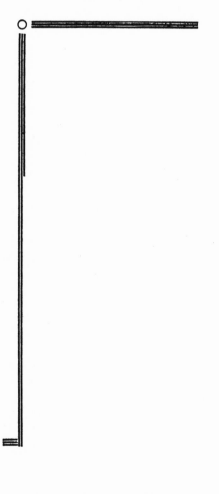

The Boys' Life of
BOBBY JONES

○ ════════════════════════════════ ○

CHAPTER I

NOT MUCH OF A START

ROBERT TYRE JONES, JR., arrived in Atlanta, Georgia, on St. Patrick's Day, 1902,
and for the first five years of his life he was about
as unpromising a prospect for a competitive athlete, not to say a champion, as could have been
selected by any of the six doctors who individually and at times collectively collaborated with
Mr. and Mrs. Jones in the effort to keep the in-
fant Jones with them. Bobby apparently was a
chronic victim of some severe digestive derange-
ment, and until he was five years old he never
managed a mouthful of solid food.

Photographs of Bobby at this time, and sundry
rather depressing descriptions, reveal him as an
almost shockingly spindling youngster with an
over-size head and legs with staring knees. If
the camera is to be trusted—and usually it is—
few youngsters at the romper age have less re-

sembled, without being actually malformed, a future athletic champion.

Bobby's first conquest, then, in the world of which he was to become the first golfing champion, was in a real battle for life itself. And it is not unreasonable to assume that he thus gained very early, and instinctively, the habit of fighting against odds without discouragement—and without feeling sorry for himself.

The popular idea, that Bobby Jones cut his teeth on a niblick and played golf from the time he could walk, is mistaken. Bobby's first love in the sporting world was baseball, and baseball was the athletic background of his family, not golf. Robert P. Jones, Bobby's father—Big Bob, he was called after Bobby, the only child, came along —was a famous outfielder at the University of Georgia; so good, indeed, that a contract with the Brooklyn Club of the old National League was waiting for him at graduation. He did not sign the contract—but that, as Mr. Kipling says, is another story which may be told later.

Big Bob never had played golf, and Bobby never had heard of it, when the family moved from the little house in Willow Street to the Corinthian Apartments, which had a vacant lot adjoining; just the kind of vacant lot on which the typical American boy of that era was to be found playing ball after school hours, and perhaps during school hours. Bobby had turned his fifth birthday and had scored a number of encouraging victories over poached eggs, farina, and the like—a vast improvement over peptonoids, certainly. And his father naturally was sympathetic with the little boy's interest in baseball; it was the game Big Bob had loved best of all, and it was good exercise.

So it comes about that some of the clearest early recollections of the boy who retired from golf as the champion of the world are mixed up with baseball; perhaps Bobby's most vivid memory of his childhood is of an organ-grinder who came around to the vacant lot one day with a monkey which could catch a ball with the most beautiful certainty.

"I envied that monkey," Bobby once confessed, with a grin. "I had a very definite wish that I could be a monkey and astonish the boys with my skill at catching a ball. I used to lie awake at night and think about how fine it would be."

Bobby started out as catcher on his team. His equipment was simple and did not include a mask. This did not keep him from working close behind the bat; it added a definite peril to the other distinctions of the position, and Bobby was proud enough of his job—until one day a batsman of the opposing team, Bob Ravenel, swung too hard at a pitched ball, the bat came all the way round, slipped from his hands, and cracked the youthful Robert on the side of his head. While this mishap did not turn him against baseball, and may not be taken as a contributory factor in his eminence in golf, it did serve to show that even at that tender age Bobby had a modicum of ability to learn from experience; he gave up his place as catcher for a position farther removed from batting range.

It was at this time, too, that Bobby started to school; the Woodbury School, populated mostly by girls, who appeared somehow very large and formidable to Bobby and the three other small boys in his department. He remembers an oppressed sort of feeling at this school, and certainly he had measles, whooping cough, and other juvenile ailments in rapid succession, so his attendance was irregular and his scholastic progress nothing to be excited about.

One day Big Bob asked him if he would rather keep on going to school, or stop and play ball.

And that, Bobby says, was quite the simplest

choice he remembers having been offered in his whole life.

Up to this time—the summer of 1907—Bobby continued to know nothing whatever about golf. He had never heard of the game. As suggested, there was no golf tradition in his family. He had no country estate on which to take up the sport, as the great Jerry Travers had in early boyhood. Indeed, Bobby's encouragement in baseball went no farther back than his father, Big Bob. His grandfather, Robert Tyre Jones, of Canton, Georgia, for whom he was named, was an old-fashioned business man of the stalwart type, with no inclination toward play himself, and no patience with those who went in for athletics. Once, when his own son, Bobby's father, was highly praised for his baseball ability—it really amounted to genius—by an authority on the game, Mr. Jones drew himself up to a singularly forbidding height and rejoined:

"You could not pay him a poorer compliment!"

And when Bobby's father was offered the Brooklyn contract, to play professional baseball after his graduation from the University, the Old Roman set his foot down right there—and one more budding career in the big leagues was flattened before it started. Bobby's grandfather never would go to see his son play baseball, during a brilliant collegiate career. And the first sporting event of any kind the Old Roman ever permitted himself to witness was on July 4, 1918, when Bobby, then beginning to achieve renown as a great kid golfer of sixteen, played with Perry Adair of Atlanta a Red Cross benefit match on his home course, East Lake, against Jimmy Standish and Kenneth Edwards.

Bobby was talking about it, years afterward.

"Dad said I ought to feel highly honored," he said, "because Grandfather never would go to watch *him* play baseball. But Grandfather never did admit that he had come down from Canton to watch me play golf. He said he had business in Atlanta that day—the Fourth of July!"

And years afterward, in 1926, when a great party from Atlanta went to New York to greet Bobby, coming home with the British open championship, his grandfather went along with the rest of the family and a hundred others. But when the reporters tried to get a story out of it from the Old Roman, he told them firmly that he had just happened to be in New York on business.

Be that as it may, I know well enough that three years earlier, in 1923, Mr. Jones was taking

6

a deep interest in the golfing exploits of his grandson. For at the Inwood Country Club on Long Island, the day the national open championship began, Bobby showed me a telegram from his grandfather.

"Keep the ball in the fairway," it read, "and make all the putts go down."

Bobby's eyes looked a bit misty as he read it.

"He doesn't know what it's all about, exactly," said Bobby. "But he's pulling for me—and that helps a lot."

How much it helped no one can say surely. But it was at Inwood that Bobby won his first major championship, in the great tournament that marked the turning point of his career from the "seven lean years" without a victory of major importance to the seven fat years in which he won thirteen national titles and became the first golfing champion of the world.

Golf came to the Joneses in the early summer of 1907. Even with baseball, Bobby wasn't picking up in health as rapidly as his parents desired, and one day Big Bob, recalling his own rugged, barefoot days in the mountains of North Georgia, announced to the assembled family, consisting of Bobby and his mother, that he was going to pull off Bobby's shoes and turn him out to grass.

7

So the little family moved five miles out of the city, to board with Mrs. Frank Meador in a big house no more than a long mashie pitch from what was then the second fairway of the East Lake golf course of the Atlanta Athletic Club.

This was a radical and a happy change for the spindling little boy. There was a stable; a garden with a lot of raspberries in it, and a reasonable supply of snakes; a small creek to be dammed for hypothetical fishing—it appears that Bobby never caught any fish, but never got over the idea that they were there to be caught—and eventually an elderly pony, which Bobby named Clara, for his mother, a compliment which, he says, Mrs. Jones never seemed properly to appreciate.

There also was Frank Meador, two years older than Bobby, and several young men, boarders, who played golf at East Lake.

One of these, Fulton Colville, deserves a niche in the Hall of Fame. He gave Bobby Jones his first golf club.

Mr. Colville was out on the front lawn one afternoon, practicing tiny run-up shots with a refractory cleek, as golfers will, and Bobby was watching him, solemnly and intently, obviously trying to get the idea.

"Want to try it, son?" Mr. Colville asked.

8

Bobby did want to, and he tried it.

It would be pleasant to record that the future world champion's first effort with a golf club was a brilliant success, but this is a true story. The club was nearly as long as Bobby; the shaft poked him woefully in the stomach—and he missed the ball altogether. And the grown-up golfer watching this historic performance, little dreaming that it *was* historic, and thinking only that the little boy in rompers presented a pathetic figure, swinging a golf club as long as himself, said he would fix that, all right. And he sawed off the shaft right under the leather grip and presented the club to Bobby with his blessing—the cleek, ever a tricky club, wasn't working well for Mr. Colville, anyway.

Now, if you fancy a sawed-off cleek was a poor kit of tools for a future champion to start his game with, you should have seen the first golf course on which Bobby Jones played. Very likely it was the worst golf course in the world, at the time, and the worst golf course that ever has been in the world. It was not really a golf course at all, but a side-road extending past the Meador home into the main highway along the East Lake property. This side-road was the fairway, a ditch along each side was the rough; the first hole was dug in the clay surface in front of the house, and the second hole was not a hole at all, but another ditch, on the farther side of the highway by the club property, not quite a hundred yards away.

It is a matter of general conviction that Bobby Jones never made a hole in one shot until 1927, at the eleventh green of the East Lake course. But some days the road fairway was dry and hard, and Bobby, with the abbreviated cleek, and Frank Meador, with an old mashie, could wallop a ball that would go rolling down a convenient rut and into the cross-ditch that was one of the two holes of the worst golf course in the world. Bobby made this ditch-hole in one shot several times before he was six years old.

So, at the age of not quite six years, Bobby Jones began playing golf with one sawed-off club on the worst course in the world; still loving baseball better; sticking to what he considered golf because there were not enough boys in the neighborhood for baseball; and dancing in the road with fury when the ball, instead of rolling into the ditch that was named a hole, took a wild bound and rolled into another ditch under a little bridge covered with briers.

Golf in this guise did not make much of an impression on Bobby—and yet his acute exaspera-

tion at missing a shot seems now to have been a
true promise of artistry, rather than mere child-
ish rage. You know, Bobby would hurl an occasional club after a missed shot as late as his
fifteenth year, and plenty of criticism it got him,
playing before big galleries in the exhibition tours
for the Red Cross war chest. And even at the very
beginning he could not endure calmly to miss a
shot he knew he could execute, the beginning of
the vast impatience of his later years with anything less than perfection in his own performance. From the beginning, Bobby never made the
mistake of being angry with an opponent in golf
—only with his own mistakes. And, as the London *Times* said editorially after his retirement
from competitive golf, today "the flames still leap
up within, though by strength of character he has
subdued a naturally fiery temper till he plays the
game outwardly as a man of ice."

While Bobby and Frank Meador were hammer-
ing disreputable-looking golf balls up and down
the roadway, Bobby's father and mother had gone
in for the game properly, taking lessons from
Jimmy Maiden, professional at the East Lake
Club, and playing regularly on that course. Nobody paid much attention to the two youngsters,
and the profoundest idea Bobby had of the game

at this period was that golf balls were easy to lose and hard to come by—and that baseball was a lot more fun. Still, he did hate terribly to miss a shot in this queer game of golf.

He resumed baseball when the family moved back into town in the fall of 1907, and learned to drive his first automobile—a toy vehicle of two-foot power called a Glasscock Racer. And the following summer, in 1908, the Joneses moved back to East Lake and directly into the club grounds, in a little cottage just back of what was then the thirteenth green of the golf course; the house is still there and is known to the older club members as the "mule house"—why, nobody seems to know.

And soon after this came the first big event in Bobby Jones's golfing career—the biggest event, perhaps. Stewart Maiden, a stocky little Scot from Carnoustie, came to East Lake to take the place of his brother, Jimmy Maiden, as golf professional. It was from Stewart Maiden that Bobby Jones learned his golfing method. When he came to East Lake, the members called the silent little fellow "Kiltie." Now, all over the world, he is known as Kiltie, the King-Maker.

Late one afternoon Bobby and his mother walked over to the gate of the club to meet Big

Bob, and there they were joined presently by Jimmy Maiden and his brother Stewart, who was to have so profound an influence on the little boy, a few months past six years of age, who stood there staring up at him. Bobby's father and mother and Jimmy Maiden did all the talking. Stewart did not say a word. And Bobby just stared at him—wondering in a vague sort of way if Stewart could talk at all.

Stewart Maiden's conversational style was monosyllabic—but his golfing style was as fine and sound as ever came out of Scotland. And it wasn't a week before a little boy in rompers— a little boy with an over-size head and staring knees—was following Stewart Maiden solemnly about the East Lake course, never minding in the least that the imperturbable Scot paid him not the slightest attention, but watching—watching— watching.

And that was the way Bobby Jones began to play golf.

CHAPTER II

BOBBY'S first rounds of golf on the regular course at East Lake were not, properly speaking, rounds at all. He accompanied his father and mother occasionally on condition that he would take only one club and would keep up with them, which he managed by the simple plan of beating the ball along and scampering after it as fast as his skinny legs would carry him. His outfit now consisted of three clubs, the faithful cleek, which invariably was the one selected when allowed to play with his parents; a brassie given him from his mother's assortment, cut down to fit; and a discarded mashie of his father's, much too long and heavy. He used the cleek as a putter when he reached the green in time to hole out with the other players. When he followed Stewart Maiden, in the matches the little professional played with members of the club, Bobby didn't

14

carry any weapons at all. He simply tagged around after Stewart and watched him solemnly.

The generally accepted idea that Bobby's first association with Stewart Maiden was in the rôle of pupil is quite wrong. Stewart never gave him a regular lesson in golf. After Bobby acquired something of a game, and began playing in tournaments and finally achieved the position of a national figure in golf, Stewart was accustomed to coach him at times, when a club wasn't working for him; and he went with Bobby to a number of important tournaments; with his own perfect style and his unusual understanding of the fundamentals of the game, Stewart almost invariably was able to straighten out the kinks in Bobby's own method, so exactly modeled on Stewart's own play.

But that was years later. In the first days, Bobby picked up his game as imitatively as a monkey, watching the man who played the best golf at the club. Bobby never was conscious of studying Stewart's method, or of trying to play like him. He liked to follow him about and watch him, because he was the best player Bobby had ever seen; he was a sort of ideal golfer, who paid no attention to little boys, but who produced beautiful golf shots and did holes in scores that amazed and delighted this particular little boy.

So Bobby would follow Stewart five or six holes, and then go back to the little house where he lived, just behind the thirteenth green of the original course at East Lake, and get out his mashie and the cleek which he used for a putter and a cap full of old balls, and go out by the thirteenth green and pitch all the balls on to it, and then go and putt them all out, over and over again.

And that, by the way, old-fashioned as the method may be, probably is the very best way for a youngster to start learning to play golf. The older professionals—the most famous competitors of a generation ago—usually learned their golf in that manner. As caddies, they did not have the use of the regular course; so they put in their spare hours, when not carrying clubs, pitching and putting—pitching and chipping and putting, at some makeshift green; gaining a style and a touch in the immensely important short-game which later became the principal advantage they enjoyed over the crack amateurs, carefully taught— usually with the wood clubs first of all, and never restricted to the humble pitching and putting of the "cramped caddies," as one writer has called them, who later became great professional players and teachers, and the masters of the game. It was in this way that Harry Vardon and James Braid and J. H. Taylor learned golf—most famous of the British professionals, who for more than twenty years were known as the Great Triumvirate.

Bobby, however, was blissfully unconscious of laying the groundwork for a game that was to carry him to the ranking of the first golfing champion of the world. He enjoyed pitching and putting all by himself; and he possessed a faculty, also without being at all aware of it, of mimicry which caused him to copy the methods of Stewart Maiden with such astonishing accuracy that when he was a stocky boy of fifteen an old friend of Stewart's, watching Bobby drive from a distant tee in a practice round before a southern amateur championship at Birmingham, inquired of the man beside him when Stewart had arrived.

It was Bobby's father he addressed.

"Stewart isn't here," was the reply.

"Oh yes, he is!" Stewart's friend insisted. "Do you think I don't recognize that old Carnoustie swing? Nobody else in the world hits a golf ball like that!"

"Nevertheless," said Big Bob, with a grin, "I

must insist that that is not Stewart Maiden, but my son Rob!"

Yet this gift of mimicry, as Bobby recalls it, never was suggested as a means to the end of developing a golfing style; it was exploited by Bobby's father for the entertainment of his own friends on the veranda of their home, when Bobby was encouraged to get out on the lawn and perform imitations of this player or that—usually some one in the gathering. There was one excellent friend of the family, Judge Broyles, who never seemed to get so much amusement out of the imitation of his own style as the others. The judge used to like to carry his own clubs, and, when preparing to play a shot, he laid the bag down carefully by his left foot, swung at the ball, and then, keeping his eyes on the flight of the ball, removed his left hand from the club, stooped, grasped the bag of clubs, and set out after the shot at a slow trot, all in one comprehensive gesture.

Bobby could imitate Judge Broyles's "follow-through," as Big Bob called it, with a ludicrous precision; he probably could do it today, more than twenty years later—all through his career he could reproduce any swing he saw, good, bad, or startling. But it was Stewart Maiden's smooth

and beautiful swing he naturally appropriated for
his own use; and, with certain minor alterations
due to a difference in physique as Bobby grew up,
that was the swing which carried him to the top
of the world.

So Bobby traveled along the pathway of golf
on a regular course, as a spindling kid in rompers;
and Big Bob got Stewart to make for him a real
set of juvenile clubs, with a little bag in which
to carry them, and the brassie he got from his
mother, and the over-size mashie his father had
discarded, and even the original cut-down cleek
which was his first weapon were discarded in
turn, and Bobby began to play the East Lake
course with Perry Adair and Frank Meador,
somewhat older than himself. Perry was the first
"boy wonder" of Dixie, later on.

And yet, when he was eight and nine years
old, Bobby was playing at least as much tennis as
golf, and doing a lot of fishing in the lake on the
club's property. And at the age of ten he and
Frank Meador, who played tennis as well as golf
with him, got into a regular competition in the
former sport—somebody suggested, as a joke,
that the kids enter the club championship in
doubles. They took the suggestion seriously, their
entry was accepted, and in the first round they

were matched with Carleton Smith and Eston Mansfield, one of the greatest teams southern tennis ever produced.

The ensuing match must have been edifying in the extreme, and quite a gallery assembled on the small green grandstand by the No. 1 court.

Smith in those days employed an odd service, a sort of modified Lawford stroke, which caused the ball to bound high and crankily. If the diminutive Bobby stood in the usual position of the receiver, at the base-line, the ball invariably bounded far over his head, and the only place from which he could reach it was with his back almost against the wire netting of the backstop, at a distance from the court where it required a hard swing to get the ball over the net in return. This at once aroused the tumultuous interest of the gallery, and when it became Bobby's turn to serve, the rooting was tremendous. His own style was modeled on that of a very large, tall expert—Ed Carter, who used a full-arm, slashing service known as the American type. When Bobby began tossing the ball high in the air and unwinding his pet idea of the American swing, the gallery encouraged him with shouts and advice:

"Hit it hard, Bob! Knock him down!"

Bobby walloped the ball as hard as he could,

and he and Frank bounded about with catlike energy, and the gallery had a wonderful time while the match lasted—which, as you may guess, was not long enough to be tiresome. And that was as far as Bobby got in tennis.

Bobby was going to school, too, in those early days when he lived in the little house on the East Lake golf course. He did not like going to school, and has confessed to a wicked plan of walking in mud puddles on the way, so he would be sent home—but that was only on days when he felt that he simply had to go fishing. It was on a fishing excursion after one of these defections that he earned the only whipping his father ever gave him. His father was late going over town that morning, and, suspecting Bobby's ruse in getting his feet wet, expressly forbade him to go fishing or to go near the lake. As soon as Big Bob departed, Bobby got out his fishing-tackle and went down to the boathouse, where there was a little dock, and started angling.

In a very few minutes he hooked the largest fish he had ever caught—nearly a foot long, it was, and to Bobby's ecstatic gaze it looked much larger. As it came up out of the water and he got a good view of it, the excitement proved too great. Instead of swinging the rod inward so he could reach the fish, he stepped right off the dock, going after it. The water was six feet deep there, and if Ed, the boathouse attendant, had not been near and hauled him out, fish and all, there is an appallingly good chance that this biography never would have been written. And that exploit gained for Bobby the first and last whipping his father ever gave him.

So Bobby's early boyhood was of a very normal, usual kind—school and fishing and tennis and baseball and golf, the baseball trending into the more individual kinds of sport, especially golf, as his parents played more and more, and most of the grown-ups whom Bobby encountered seemed to talk about that game more than others. He was always a good student, barring the early foot-wetting episodes, and went steadily along through the primary and grade schools—his health, greatly benefited by his outdoor activity, now being sound—got through Technological High School in three years, and entered the Georgia School of Technology at sixteen, being graduated in the hardest course at that institution, mechanical engineering, at twenty.

Bobby settled down into golf as his favorite game about the age of nine, when he won the junior championship of his home club, at East

Lake. But to trace his competitive career, we must go back three years, to the days before he lived within the precincts of the East Lake golf course, when he and his parents were boarding at Mrs. Meador's home across the street from the club, and there was a small party given for four tiny golfers, and a tournament with a real cup for a prize.

Mrs. Meador arranged the tournament for the party. The competition was over six holes on the old East Lake course; and the other contestants were Perry Adair, Frank Meador, and Alexa Stirling, a little red-headed girl who was beginning the study of golf under the instruction of Stewart Maiden—she later won the national championship of the United States three times in succession.

The tournament planned by Mrs. Meador was at medal play; six holes, the lowest aggregate score to win. And Bobby was awarded the cup, though his recollection to this day is that Alexa should have won it. Frank Meador, however, was keeping score, and he insisted that Bobby was the victor, and as his mother was giving the party, Frank was regarded as having a sort of plenary connection with the tournament, so the little cup, three inches tall, was awarded to Bobby, the

23

youngest of the quartet. Bobby took it to bed with him that night. It was the first of one hundred and twenty cups and vases and platters and pitchers that he won by the time he was twenty and stopped playing in invitation tournaments. So it is, in a way, historical. And of all the collection there's one little cup that never is allowed to go unpolished—and Bobby never slept with another one!

The next tournament in which Bobby took part was nearly two years later, and it was a matchplay affair, in which the contestants were handicapped according to age. Mrs. E. G. Ballenger promoted this tournament, over the complete course at East Lake, and Bobby got into the final round with Perry Adair, who, being older, had to give him one stroke as handicap in each of the two rounds—the match was played at the same distance as the final match in a national championship, 36 holes.

The match was played on Sunday, and the two youngsters felt immensely important as the other players on the course stood politely aside to let them go through—they were playing a "tournament match," you see. At that, it is not to be inferred that they held anybody up unduly. They had not reached the stage where they studied their

shots and inspected the line of each putt micro-
scopically. Their method was simple and direct—
and rapid. They walked up to the ball and socked
it, through the fairway and occasionally the
rough. And when they got to the green they let
the line of the putt take care of itself—their idea
of putting was the one set down by George Duncan, the great Scottish professional:

"You just go up to the ball and knock it into
the hole!"

No, the boys didn't delay the game for other
players on the course. And Bobby grew up to be
one of the promptest golfers the game has known.
When he got along to where everything he did in
golf was a matter of importance to the world of
sport, Bobby never lost an opportunity to advise
against taking too much time over a shot. His
idea was, and is, much in accord with that of
Hamlet, that the native hue of resolution is all
too likely to be sicklied o'er with a pale cast of
thought; though Bobby expresses it differently.
He says you can't keep your concentration
screwed up very long at a time, if you really
are concentrating on a stroke; it's better, he says,
to make your mind up concerning the shot before you take your stance, and then hit the ball
while the decision is fresh and strong.

Bobby and Perry did a lot of rapid playing, and very little thinking, in their big match; and Bobby won, 2-1, at the thirty-fifth green. It was a little vase he got, this time.

So his competitive career was fairly launched, beginning at the age of six—and he won the first two tournaments in which he played. It was still a long, long way to the championship phase of the game, and it is proper to say here that Bobby never came to regard the winning of titles, even major titles, as the great thing in life, or even in sport. Many times in his brilliant career, and sometimes at its various peaks of conquest, he has spoken to me of his longing for the day when he could "hang up the clubs," so far as the championships were concerned, and go back as far as might be along the trail to the good old days when golf was only a game, to be played for the fun of it.

"Though, of course," he said once, "it can never be again what it was when Alexa and Perry and I first played it."

There's nothing in the world like the fierce glare of championship to take the early dew off the turf!

CHAPTER III

THE first championship won by Bobby Jones was at the age of nine years, and it was, as you may guess, not a very large or important championship. Still, it was a formal tournament, regulated in all respects like grown-up tournaments; the junior championship of the Atlanta Athletic Club, whose golf course was at East Lake, the home club and the home course of the future world's champion throughout his career, though he later became a member, honorary or regular, of so many clubs in all parts of the world that he probably could not tell you the names of all of them, or even how many there were. Bobby did not meet his friend Perry Adair in this tournament; Perry was in the other bracket, or section of the pairings, and was defeated by Howard Thorne in the semi-final round, while Bobby was working his way through another competitor, to meet Howard in the final match, at 36 holes. Howard was relatively quite a big boy; he was sixteen years old, and naturally he could hit a ball a lot farther than Bobby. But the patient practice about the old thirteenth green, back of the "mule house," now began to show up in Bobby's game; he was amazingly accurate when he arrived within reach of the green, and his steady pitching and putting proved too much for the more powerful but less accurate Howard, who was defeated 5-4.

Bobby was awarded a big cup, along with the title of junior champion; at least, it seemed like a big cup to him. And soon afterward his picture was printed in the *American Golfer*. That same picture has been reprinted a number of times, since—once after Bobby had won the British and the American open championships in 1926, along with a picture made at the same age of Jess Sweetser, who won the British amateur title that year.

"They hold all the major championships there are," read the caption; for Bobby at the time also held the American amateur championship of 1925, that in 1926 not having been played when the funny little photographs were printed.

But you may be sure that Bobby was much

prouder, the first time. The cut portrays a scrubby, towsled-haired youngster, still with skinny arms and legs; just a typical American small boy about halfway through grade school. You could pick out dozens of boys at any recess period who looked a lot more like championship prospects at golf or any other sport, though it is unlikely that any one of the dozens, or any boy of that age you could find in all the world, could swing a golf club as the youthful Bobby was swinging it then. The picture, however, indicates a somewhat flatter method than he employed later, when his style became an international concern as the "glass of fashion and the mold of form."

Still, it was a very good and sound little swing, though it did not carry him to a successful defense of his title as junior champion in the tournament the following year. The difference in age between Bobby and his great friend and rival, Perry Adair, was beginning to tell. Perry was three years older, and in 1912, when Bobby was ten, Perry won the club's junior title, defeating Howard Thorne in the finals after Howard had got revenge on Bobby for the previous licking by beating him in the semi-final round.

Perry was beginning to be noticed in the papers. Two years later he was regarded as the Boy

Wonder of Dixie, when, at the age of fifteen, he went to the final round of the southern amateur championship, defeating his father, George Adair, on the way, and losing to Nelson Whitney of New Orleans at the finish. Three years later, when Bobby was thirteen and Perry was sixteen, and Bobby had grown to be somewhat larger and stronger than his great little rival, there began one of the most remarkable competitions in the annals of American golf; the boys met at home and afield, in invitation tournaments and friendly matches, and there is no way of knowing just how much this long and brilliantly contested struggle meant to Bobby's future development and career. But it is certain that through the first state championship, in 1916, when Bobby at last gained definitely the upper hand, his association with Perry Adair and his father, and the encouragement given him by the latter, and the sharp battles accorded him by the former, were the leading factors in Bobby's development.

At this time, however, Bobby being ten years old, he was playing the old original course at East Lake around 90, and occasionally a stroke or two better—and it may be explained that the old course at East Lake was an exceedingly tough scoring proposition. It was an odd affair, laid out,

BOBBY STARTING GOLF AT AGE OF SIX
—EAST LAKE

BOBBY AT NINE, WINNING HIS FIRST TITLE, JUNIOR
CHAMPIONSHIP, ATLANTA ATHLETIC CLUB

I believe, by Tom Bendelow; there were only two par-3 holes on it, the first and the third, so that after progressing that far a back-breaking stretch of fifteen holes confronted the hopeful golfer without a single short hole, most of the fifteen being of the long two-shot variety—the hardest type of hole in golf. The course was altered in 1914, after George Adair and Stewart Maiden came back from a tour of all the famous golf courses in Great Britain—Mr. Adair took Perry along— and while a number of the original holes were retained the general plan was radically changed; it is many yards longer than the original layout, but, on the whole, easier to score on. So you may understand that cards running regularly close to 90 were astonishingly good, on a difficult golf course, by a skinny little boy ten years old. East Lake members were beginning to talk about "Little Bob" Jones, and occasionally you might see a paragraph in the sporting pages of the papers concerning him. But Perry was more in the limelight the next three or four years.

It was in 1913, the year before the East Lake course was redesigned, that two things happened to Bobby which now appear worthy of mention as influencing his outlook on golf and his subsequent attitude toward the game.

Up to this time, as suggested previously, Bobby had been taking his golf as an incidental amusement, along with tennis and fishing and baseball. It was just another game, and his attitude toward it was purely and personally competitive—he was always playing against somebody, trying to beat somebody, just as in tennis or in baseball, and if he succeeded in beating his opponent he felt a sense of achievement. Even when engaged in medal competition—that is, where the entire field play for the best aggregate score—Bobby always was trying to beat the score of Perry Adair, or of whoever seemed to be the most dangerous competitor. So far as I can learn, while he kept carefully the score of every round of golf he played, he never regarded the score itself as anything but a sort of detached record. He was playing always against a definite, personal opponent. In a word, he was playing golf against *somebody*, not against *something*.

And this may appear at first as an unimportant matter, so I am going rather particularly into the beginning of Bobby's change of attitude toward the game, a change that was just ten years in the making—a change from personal to impersonal golf, which was the foundation for a record that, in all human probability, will stand forever unequaled.

This change, which required so many years and so many heartaches to complete, began in the late summer of 1913, when Harry Vardon and Ted Ray, the great English professionals, came to play an exhibition match at East Lake, following the national open championship at Brookline. That tournament itself had an influence on Bobby's golfing ideas. It was the first time that golf definitely established its major competitions on the front page of American newspapers—for Vardon and Ray had finished in a triple tie with a Boston boy of nineteen, an amateur named Francis Ouimet, and the youngster had beaten them both in the play-off, and saved our big cup from going overseas. Bobby had read about this achievement, by another boy—a much older boy, of course, but still a boy—and suddenly he began to feel that golf was a real game, a big game, which got into the headlines, just like a world series in baseball.

And then, in the course of a tour of the country, Vardon and Ray came to Atlanta, along in October, and played a match at Bobby's home club, with Stewart Maiden and the late Willie Mann, then professional at the Druid Hills Golf Club of Atlanta; a beautifully contested match in which big Ted Ray had to sink an eight-foot putt at the thirty-sixth green to win the contest for his side, 1 up.

It was Bobby's first opportunity to watch famous golfers in action; Vardon had won the British open championship five times; he won it once more, in 1914; and Ray was British champion in 1912. And Bobby followed every step of the 36 holes.

Bobby has confessed since that what most impressed him at the time was the tremendous driving of big Ted Ray, the longest hitter of that era, and a miraculous sort of pitch executed by Ray, playing the twelfth hole of the afternoon round. He remembers a gigantic wallop of Ray's that went clear over the fifth green, when all the others were short; and another which sailed and rolled 320 yards, nearly down to the old thirteenth green, back of the "mule house"—the same old green at which Bobby in the earliest days of his golf had pitched and putted through many a long afternoon. And best of all he remembers the shot over the tree, going to the twelfth hole.

This shot, being a matter of golfing history, merits description. I too was in the gallery, and in thirty-four years of golf I never have seen another one like it.

34

The Atlanta professionals had finished the morning round 2 down, but had started brilliantly after luncheon and soon were in the lead. Then, beginning with this twelfth hole, the Englishmen executed four birdies in succession and went out in front again. It was Vardon who got the birdie 3 at the twelfth; but Ray's performance in getting his par 4 was what everybody in that gallery was talking about later.

Ted's drive, as usual, was well in front of the others, but the ball was somewhat shoved out to the right and stopped with a tree exactly in the line to the green. The tree was about forty feet in height, the foliage was thick, and Ray's ball was no more than fifty feet from it, the green being fully 170 yards away. A shot for the green looked simply hopeless—a long chance at slicing the ball around one side of the tree, or pulling around the other. As for shooting over the tree, no one even considered that.

Big Ted lumbered along up to the ball, puffing contentedly away on his famous pipe—he always smoked a pipe while playing—and took one look at the ball, one look at the tree, and one look at the distant green. Then he pulled a mashie-niblick from the bag—a much-lofted club designed to pitch the ball no farther than 140 yards at most—

and he hit that ball just as hard as he could, knocking it down (as the saying is) to impart backspin and raise the ball quickly and sharply into the air.

Up flew a divot, nearly as large as Ted's ample foot. Up also came the ball, fairly buzzing with the terrific spin—almost straight up, it seemed, towering over that tree, climbing like a rocket, and sailing at the height of an office-building, until it was over the green, on which it dropped lightly and with no roll at all.

Only a few times have I seen a gallery so affected by a golf shot. Men pounded each other on the back, and shouted and crowed and cackled with delight and amazement. And old Ted, puffing away again at the inevitable pipe, was striding after the ball, long before it came down. As I recall it, he did not even watch it landing on the green.

Naturally, the eager little boy, dodging about in the big gallery, would remember that shot as long as he lived. And Bobby often speaks of it today; he says it is the greatest shot he ever saw.

But when the match was all over, and when Vardon and Ray had played the Mackenzie brothers the next day at the Brookhaven course of the Capital City Club, after the great professionals had gone, Bobby began to think more and more about the smooth, beautiful playing of Harry Vardon, the Old Master; and how, on two courses he never had seen before, Harry had scored 72-72-73-71 in four consecutive rounds, a total of 288 strokes, an exact average of 4's, all the way.

An average of 4's—Bobby got something of an idea out of that. Even the kid of eleven began to think, in a vague sort of way, that if you could just keep scoring an average of 4's you could win almost anything—almost any match—almost any tournament.

I was talking with him about the beginning of this idea, many years later, when he was in the thick of his championship career.

"I wouldn't qualify that estimate the least bit, today," he said. "I'll be glad to take the 4's, any time and anywhere!"

It is a rather singular fact that of the eleven American open championships, and the four British, in which Bobby has competed, an average of 4's would have won him all fifteen. Of the fifteen, Bobby won seven. But he was better than 4's only twice—he scored 285 in the British open in 1927, and 287 in his final American open, in 1930. And an average of 4's, or 288, would have won either of them for him.

It seemed to the eleven-year-old youngster, scampering about in the gallery at East Lake that bright October day, that old Harry, shooting par golf all the way, was playing against something beside his visible opponents, Stewart Maiden and Willie Mann; something that Bobby couldn't see; something that kept old Harry serious and sort of separate and far away from the gallery and his opponents and even his big partner; he seemed to be playing against something or some one not in the match at all. And he seemed to be playing all alone.

But long before Bobby ever got it straightened out in his own mind, something else happened, soon after the big exhibition match, and curiously connected with Bobby's impressions of it, though Bobby did not know it.

Bobby shot an 80 on the old course at East Lake, for the first time.

He was playing, as usual, with Perry Adair. And for once—for the first time, he wasn't paying any attention to what Perry was doing, or if he was beating Perry or Perry was beating him. Bobby was scoring better than he ever had scored before, and he had no room in his mind to think of anything else. At the last green he was left with a four-foot putt for an even 80, which he never had done before. . . . He must have wondered why his skinny little chest was so tight and why his hands were trembling as he stood up to that putt, which was not to beat Perry, but just to score an 80 on the card. . . . Down it went! And on the card went the 80. And also on the card went Perry's name, signed on the line marked "Attested."

And away across the East Lake golf course went Bobby Jones, setting off at a brisk trot to find his dad. Bobby found Big Bob at the fourteenth green. He was putting. Bobby had sense enough not to disturb him until that delicate process was completed. Then he walked solemnly up to Big Bob and held out the card, without a word —his hand still was trembling. Big Bob took the card and looked at it. Then he looked at Bobby. Then he put his arms around Bobby and hugged him—hard. And Bobby doesn't remember what Big Bob said. But he remembers that Big Bob's eyes were wet.

And so, before he was a dozen years old, Bobby Jones had discovered a new adversary in golf, the Great Opponent whose tangible form is only a card and pencil; he had played his first round against the toughest foeman of them all—Old Man Par.

CHAPTER IV

THE FIRST MINOR CHAMPIONSHIP

IN VIEW of the extreme importance of the influence of Old Man Par on Bobby Jones's attitude toward competitive golf, beginning when he was eleven years old, and exerted with a gradually increasing emphasis throughout his career, it may be as well here to explain just what par is, in golf.

The term may be defined as correct scoring for each of the eighteen holes of a golf course. It is based on the length of the hole and the known range of the expert player's shots, with a standard allotment of two putts for each green. There is, naturally, a considerable difference in the measurements of par for women, which are shorter than those for men. All references to par in this narrative are, of course, to the masculine variety, which is based on the following scale:

A hole up to 250 yards, par 3.

From 251 to 450 yards, par 4.

From 451 yards upward, par 5.

Correct play, then, for a par 3 hole involves reaching the green with one shot and holing out in two putts; for a par 4, reaching the green with the second shot; and for a par 5, reaching the green with the third shot. Of course there is infinite variation in the manner of achieving a par score on any hole. On a par-4 hole, for example, a player may miss three shots hopelessly and then sink an approach of a hundred yards. This is by no means perfect golf, yet the 4 on the card counts exactly the same. A number of par-4 holes have been made in a single shot; and many thousands of the shorter par-3 holes. One well-known professional, Sandy Herd of Scotland, has done eighteen holes in a single shot for each, during a career of nearly forty years. He is believed to hold the record for this combination of skill and fortune. At the time of his retirement from competitive golf, Bobby Jones had done only one hole in one shot—the eleventh hole of his home course, East Lake, a par 3 of 175 yards. This was in 1927, when he had been playing golf nearly twenty years.

But if the means of achieving par scores are devious, the consistent adding of one par hole to another is as certain as anything can be in this uncertain world, and especially in such a game as golf, to bring about winning results in the long run. And long runs of par never have been, and never will be, achieved by wild or inexpert play aided by good luck. The cold figures on the card, except in the most unusual circumstances, are good enough to win major competitions on courses of championship caliber; and the competitor with the game and the heart and the infinite patience to move along step by step with Old Man Par will never find himself outside the front rank at the finish of any major competition, and rarely indeed as low as second place.

Cards for virtually all American courses bear par figures along with the yardage of the holes. In Great Britain, the custom is not so prevalent, though of late years it has been coming into vogue. Our British cousins for many years had a fancy for "bogie" figures—the score which a good golfer might be expected to make on a hole, usually from six to ten strokes higher than American par for the round. On many seaside courses, or links, in the British Isles an inflexible par rating is absurd, by reason of the almost inevitable wind and its changes of direction. At old St. Andrews, most famous of the world's golf courses, par for the card, based on the American system of yardage, is 73. But it would be rather silly to print the figures on the card, for a hole which in one round might be easy to reach with a drive and a pitch, in the next round might be well beyond the range of two of the hardest shots with the wood.

Still, with all the variations of golf courses and wind and weather, Old Man Par seems settled pretty definitely at an average of 4's all over the world. There are great courses with a measured par ranging from 69 to 73—major championships have been played on them. But for plain, hard, uncompromising competitive purposes, the card of 72, the average of 4's, may be taken as the tangible standard and the marching pace of Old Man Par. And as long as you keep step with him—well, you're good.

Following Bobby Jones's first conscious combat—or, rather, semi-conscious combat—with Old Man Par on the original course at East Lake, when he returned a certified card of 80 against an extremely difficult par of 73, the course was redesigned radically and the new course (now known as the old one, since another has been opened) was put in play in 1914. Bobby felt distinctly homesick for a while. He reached his twelfth birthday in March of that year, and he

43

never had played golf anywhere else, and the old course was a left-handed affair—that is, you traveled around it from left to right, like the hands of a clock, and the new course went counter-clockwise, as in most modern layouts.

The big change in the East Lake course was the most memorable event in golf for Bobby, in 1914. His competition in club tournaments was without notable results, though from one of them came a funny story which went the rounds of the Atlanta newspaper offices and seems important to me because it was the first time I had heard anything really definite about Little Bob Jones. I had returned to Atlanta from Kansas City in 1913.

With the *Atlanta Journal* at that time was a man named Milt Saul, a member of the East Lake Club, who rather fancied himself at golf. He was playing in a tournament at the club, and he was discussing his progress one day with Major John S. Cohen, editor of the *Journal*, also something of a golfer.

"They really ought not to allow these kids in the tournaments," Mr. Saul said. "There are three or four in this one. I've got to play one of them, tomorrow—that Little Bob Jones, a little squirt about twelve years old. Of course I'll beat him, but what's the good of taking up time beating children?"

That was all Major Cohen heard from Mr. Saul about the East Lake affair, for some days. Then the Major asked him how the match with Little Bob came out.

Mr. Saul blushed.

"He licked me, 6-5," he confessed. "I still think I was right—they ought not to allow these kids in regular tournaments!"

After that I used to pay a bit more of attention to the kids on the East Lake course, but the principal impression I gained was that it seemed odd to see a couple of youngsters like Little Bob Jones and Frank Meador shooting golf that would defeat most of the grown men in the club—and squabbling excitedly about the ice-cream soda they had wagered on the match! It was the following year that I really began to think about Bobby Jones as a golfer.

Through 1914, then, and during the change from the old course to the new, Bobby kept plugging along, playing a lot of golf, getting into tournaments whenever he could, and still following Stewart Maiden around rather frequently, to watch him play. By this time Stewart was taking sufficient notice of him to give him a gruff tip

once in a while, a short word of advice. And he
had made for Bobby a good set of clubs, as Bobby
outgrew the juvenile outfit originally provided.
Bobby also had acquired a varied taste in golf
balls. Up to this period, a golf ball was a golf ball
to Bobby; they were all round, unless they had
been punished severely, and one was like another.
He never had played with the gutta-percha ball,
of course, and at that time never had heard of it.
The rubber-cored or lively ball which supplanted
the solid and unresilient old gutty, went on the
market in 1902, the year Bobby was born; the
first ones were named for their inventor, the Haskell, and the first ball with which Bobby played
after he became aware that there were different
kinds was a Haskell Whiz, marked with a little
blue circle. Bobby liked that ball a lot for a time,
and then, being experimentally inclined, he
switched to the Dunlop Bramble, and then the
Zome Zodiac, the latter name apparently fascinat-
ing him. He developed theories in golf ballistics,
too, when he also discovered that some balls were
larger than others, and that some of the smaller
ones were heavier than the larger projectiles. This
was long before the days of standardized sizes
and weights.

Working along lines indicated by this discov-

THE DIXIE TEAM IN THE WESTERN AMATEUR—MEMPHIS, 1920
—AND THE OLYMPIC TROPHY
(Left to right—Bobby Jones, Pollack Boyd, Perry Adair, and
Tom Prescott)

PLAYING IN WAR RELIEF MATCHES—1917
(Bobby Jones driving. In rear, left to right—Jack Hobens, Nipper
Campbell, Perry Adair)

ery, Bobby used to play two different brands of ball when the wind was blowing—a small heavy ball from the tee on holes against the wind, usually a Black Circle, and a larger and lighter ball, the Black Domino, with the wind.

Some years later the golf associations of Great Britain and the United States, perceiving that smaller and heavier balls, wound under great tension, were making such long shots possible by the experts that famous golf courses all over the world were becoming too easy, and others were being stretched to unreasonable dimensions, adopted a standard size and weight for all competitions under association control—1.62 inches in diameter and 1.62 ounces in weight. A ball might be either larger or lighter, or both, but it might not be smaller or heavier. This standard was adhered to in both the great golfing countries until January 1, 1931, when the United States Golf Association, after more than six years of deliberation and experiment, changed its standard to a larger and lighter ball, 1.68 inches in diameter and 1.55 ounces in weight. The Royal and Ancient Golf Club of St. Andrews, the British ruling body, did not concur in the change, so that as this is written a rather remarkable situation exists—our golfers, competing in Great

47

Britain, may use either the United States standard ball or the British standard, since ours is larger and lighter, while British players in the United States must change to our standard.

However Bobby may have exploited fancies in the golf balls of that era—their names are scarcely remembered now—he made excellent progress in the development of his game. He also was gaining in weight and strength, and the following year, 1915, he was deemed good enough by his father to be permitted to play in two big invitation tournaments away from home and in the southern amateur championship at his home course, East Lake. He finished up this eventful year by winning two club titles, but they came after the first important minor competition of his career.

Bobby's first tournament away from home, at the age of thirteen, was the annual invitation affair at Montgomery, Ala., at that time one of the leading events in southern golf. George Adair was taking his son Perry to Montgomery with him, and he persuaded Big Bob to let Bobby go too. Perry was playing fine golf by this time, and reached the finals with his father—who defeated him, and then went around looking as if he had lost his best friend.

Bobby's own début away from home was nothing to get excited about. Apparently he had forgotten all about Old Man Par in the qualifying round, and that fine 80 he had done at East Lake two years before; he failed to get into the first flight, of sixteen players, and in the second flight he played only moderately well, winning his way to the last round, where he was defeated by a competitor named Hickman who played golf left-handed. To Bobby, who was beginning to think pretty well of his game, it seemed adding insult to injury to get in the second flight and then be beaten by a man who stood on the wrong side of the ball.

Here was another evidence of the impatience with anything short of first-class performance that later brought Bobby's game nearer to perfection than that of any other golfer in history. He went back to Atlanta with no idea at all that his father would permit him to enter the southern amateur championship, even though it was to be played at his home club, because of his depressing showing at Montgomery. Big Bob had promised him that he might play in the southern when he was fifteen, provided he had made sufficient progress; and Bobby now was just as certain that his progress was insufficient as that he lacked

49

nearly two years of being fifteen. So he was vastly surprised when Big Bob told him he might put in his entry for the big sectional tournament —surprised and abashed; and when the committee named him as a member of the four-man team to represent the Atlanta Athletic Club in the team competition of the qualifying round, he was overwhelmed. The other members were George Adair and his son Perry, and Will Rowan. Perry was now sixteen and a seasoned competitor, who had gone to the final round of the same championship the year before; and Bobby was so nervous and burdened with responsibility that, as he later confessed, he kept looking at the ground to keep from falling over his feet.

This round, too, was epochal. Bobby's own idea was that he was playing terribly. But once again he was not playing against some visible opponent; he was at grips with Old Man Par; and he came in with a card of 83, the best score on the Atlanta Athletic Club team (which won the team prize) and a single stroke back of Charlie Dexter of Dallas and Nelson Whitney of New Orleans, then southern champion, who tied for the medal with the best scores of the field, 82. Everybody praised Bobby and told him he had won the team match for his club, and that it was a great round

—which, in those days, it was. But proud and happy as he was, Bobby couldn't help thinking of the shots he hadn't hit quite as well as he should, and of putts that should have dropped and didn't. He was happy—but he wasn't satisfied with that round. . . . Sometimes I think he never has been quite satisfied with any round he ever played.

So now Bobby was fairly launched—for there was no doubt now that it was to be golf, in the realm of sports, from that time on. At the age of thirteen years and three months, just through grade school, and the youngest player in a big sectional championship, Bobby had qualified third in a field of more than a hundred of the best amateur golfers in Dixie. Whether or not he was satisfied with his showing in the grapple with the iron certitudes of Old Man Par, his score had won the team trophy for his club, and was second only to the man who was then southern champion, and the man who was to win the title of 1915. He was in the championship. And he had established for himself a precedent—though he certainly did not suspect it at the time—of never failing to qualify in any important tournament in which he was entered.

In those days the qualifying round of the

southern amateur placed 64 competitors in the first round of match-play, at 18 holes, and this match divided the field into two divisions of 32. In this preliminary match-round Bobby defeated a man named Patterson, from Charlotte, N. C., and thus remained in the championship division. But not for long. In the second round he encountered a famous figure in southern golf, Commodore Bryan Heard of Houston, Texas, the oldest man in the tournament; a short, stocky player with grizzled hair topped by a sun helmet; a rugged and experienced veteran of a hundred tourneys, who played with a short, flat swing that sent the ball out with a low flight, tremendous run, and amazingly accurate direction. He was a wonderful putter, too; a hard man for anybody to beat, though he was at that time well past fifty. Indeed, he proved quite too hard for Bobby, though the youngster put up a desperate battle which went to the seventeenth green, where the Commodore, grim and impassive as a Chinese idol, ended the bout with a victory, 2-1.

One of the clearest memories I have of Bobby Jones is of his face, flushed brick red and curiously set, for the face of so young a boy, as he walked on to the seventeenth green, watched the Commodore sink the finishing putt, and then, his expression relaxing into a wide, boyish smile, went up to his conqueror and held out his hand.

"Did he give you a fight?" I asked the Commodore, after Bobby was out of earshot, on his way to the clubhouse.

The Commodore removed the old sun helmet and mopped his brow.

"Did he?" the Commodore repeated. "I had a par 3 left for a 76 when the match ended—that's all." He appeared to meditate a moment. Then—"He's going to be a great golfer, that boy," added Commodore Heard. "One of the greatest. Maybe *the* greatest."

CHAPTER V

BOBBY'S defeat at the hands of the Commodore placed him in the second flight of the southern amateur championship of 1915, and there he encountered three very large competitors, the shortest of whom was six feet two inches in height. The first one was Clarence Knowles of Atlanta, known as Moose Knowles; he was six feet three and weighed 220 pounds, and he was the longest driver in the south at the time. It made an odd contrast, the stumpy schoolboy of thirteen, very red in the face and very much in earnest, battling in succession with these three gigantic musketeers, but one way and another he beat them all. His match with the Moose went to the nineteenth green. Moose was outdriving the schoolboy forty and fifty yards, and on the extra hole Bobby was at least that far behind from the tee. He couldn't reach the green with his second

54

shot, indeed; but Moose missed it also, and Bobby stuck a short pitch almost against the pin, to win the hole and the match with a par 4.

Getting by the Three Musketeers—all as big as Porthos—Bobby went into the finals of the second flight with Frank Clarke of Nashville, who did a round of 76 in the morning—the match was at 36 holes—a new amateur course record, and had Bobby 3 down when they went into luncheon.

Bobby continued to fight hard in the afternoon round, but Clarke had increased his lead to 4 up as they started the last nine. The red-faced schoolboy then discharged a blast of the golf that in after years fairly blew many a determined opponent off the course; he won the next four holes in brilliant succession, squaring the match.

Long afterward Bobby was accounting for his subsequent defeat in this match, and his manner was just a bit shamefaced.

"It was just like a dumb kid," he said. "I learned in the next ten years what a foolish thing it is ever to pat yourself on the back while a match or a tournament is still going, or ever to shake hands with yourself before you shake hands with your opponent. After winning those four holes in a row, I was all set up and sure I was going to win. I remember thinking how glad I was that mother and dad were in the gallery, and how proud they must be of me."

And then Frank Clarke in his turn won the next two holes and was back in the lead, with only three more left to play. This was a terrific jolt for Bobby, the more so as he had allowed himself to get into a complacent frame of mind during his own spurt. But he rallied gamely and sank a chip-shot from off the green at the next hole, only to see his opponent drop a 30-foot putt for the half. Another half at the following hole ended the match, 2-1. Bobby had done a 78, and mother and dad told him they were proud of him. But Bobby was not at all proud of himself. He watched Charlie Dexter defeat Nelson Whitney for the championship, at 36 holes, 2 up, and he did a good deal of thinking, but he said little.

Bobby was just beginning to make a discovery —that there were two kinds of golf in the world; golf, and tournament golf, and that they were not so much alike as you might fancy.

Anyway, his self-esteem was more than a few points off when Big Bob told him, not long after the southern, that he might enter the big invitation tournament at the Roebuck Country Club of Birmingham. Here he created another sensation by winning the tournament from a field nearly as good as had played in the southern. He defeated Perry Adair in the second round, 2-1; Big Bob Jones disposed of Rube Bush of New Orleans—one of the most stylish players the south ever produced—in the same round, perhaps the best match Bobby's dad ever played in an important competition; and Bobby finally went into the final round with Bill Badham, a former Yale golfer. The match was at 18 holes, and Bobby, shooting very good golf, became more and more puzzled when the former college star kept sticking to him. They were all square at the end of the round, but this time Bobby was not at all complacent; he kept on bearing down, as the saying is, and at the third extra hole—the twenty-first of the match—he stuck a pitch-shot stone dead and won the match with a neat birdie.

The Roebuck affair was important in Bobby's career for two reasons. It was the first big tournament he won, and it inspired Big Bob to send the youngster to nearly every important invitation tournament in that part of Dixie during the rest of 1915 and 1916. For a boy thirteen and fourteen years old this, of course, was invaluable experience in competitive golf and in the development and adjustment of his game to its requirements. All the tournaments, however, came within his school vacations; golf competition never was allowed to interrupt scholastic work or to interfere with it, even when Bobby later was touring the country in exhibition matches for the American Red Cross war chest, or playing in major championships during his college days.

There is another thing it is as well to understand here. Bobby was not the son of a wealthy man. Big Bob at this time was a young lawyer in very modest circumstances, and it was a real sacrifice for him to send the boy about to tournaments, even at the moderate expense necessitated by the neighborly little events in that part of the south.

"But it never seemed anything of a sacrifice," Big Bob told me, many years later. "Rob was our only child. He was a good son—no man ever had a better. Golf was the game he loved, and it became the ambition of his mother and myself to see him progress in it, and to help him all we could. I do not remember that he ever asked me to send him to any tournament away from home. He was happy when he could go, but never unhappy when he could not. And I think he never was so eager to go as we were to send him."

So Big Bob was greatly pleased and not a little excited over Bobby's victory at Roebuck, and his subsequent triumphs at home that summer. Bobby won the Davis and Freeman Cup tournament at East Lake, and then the club championship, and, a bit later, the Druid Hills club championship, breaking the course record with a 73 and winning his first gold medal. That is one trophy missing from his collection today. He lost it on the same course later in the year; found it by the simple but laborious process of going with two caddies over every shot he had played in the round; lost it again, and never found it.

Though he was winning club championships and invitation tournaments at the age of thirteen, Bobby was still very much of a schoolboy in his attitude toward the game and his conquests. I have seen an old snapshot of him and his victim in the Druid Hills club championship—a huge chap named Archer Davidson, at least a foot taller than Bobby, a rather chunky kid wearing a white sailor hat. Bobby's expression is no less than beaming; he is the picture of complacency, and underneath Mr. Davidson's portrait is scrawled in a schoolboy hand, "The Runner-Up," while below Bobby's is, "The Champion."

And yet Bobby continued at this time to have other interests than golf. Along with that funny little old photograph were three others, different views of a windmill some two feet in height, made from one of those toy construction outfits. And each photograph was carefully labeled in the same schoolboy hand, "Windmill, Made By R. T. Jones, Jr." He seems to have had a mechanical turn of mind at the time, when he was about getting into Technological High School.

Bobby started one of his most eventful golfing years, 1916, by achieving the age of fourteen and acquiring a good many pounds in weight and a prolonged attack of lumbago, which afflicted him soon after his first tournament of the season, the Montgomery invitation. There he met Perry Adair in the semi-final round, in the most spectacular of the many matches they played, and particularly interesting because it was in this season that Bobby gradually caught up with Perry, three years his senior, to share with the little blond gamecock of Druid Hills the ranking of the kid wonders of Dixie.

In the Montgomery bout, Bobby played the first nine holes in 33 strokes; a brilliant burst of golf which had Perry 3 down and caused Bobby not unreasonably to feel that he had the match in hand. What happened on the last nine was another notable contribution to Bobby's long and arduous education in tournament golf. Perry came back in

33, including a stroke lost by a stymie at the sixteenth green, and he won that match, 1 up. It very likely was the greatest golf match played up to that time in the south—and it was played by boys of fourteen and seventeen.

Not at all depressed by Bobby's defeat in this brilliant battle, Big Bob sent him along to Knoxville a bit later, to play in the Cherokee Club's invitation tournament, and it was there that Bobby suffered most from lumbago—with curious results, as affecting his play. At this period Bobby's work with the irons and the pitching tools was extraordinarily fine and accurate; but he loved to wallop the ball from the tee; he hit great drives in range, but he never was sure where the ball was going. At Knoxville, his back was so weak and painful from the lumbago that he had to walk sideways down the steeper hills on the course, and he simply could not "let out" at the big shots; he was compelled to swing easily, the ball usually ended neatly on the fairway, and he won the Cherokee event handily, shooting a fine 73 in the last round. After that tournament he had a couple of weeks of violet-ray treatment for the lumbago, which departed, never to return; he got his big drives back, along with the wildness that occasionally made them a source of disaster, and went over to Birmingham for another tourney, at the Country Club this time, where he went along easily to the final match, in which he defeated Jack Allison 2 up, with a card of 69—one of his best rounds in competition to that time, over a tricky though not especially difficult course.

It was in this tournament, by the way, that Bobby gained the impression that a hole made in one shot was not necessarily an indication of great golfing ability. A friend of his, Webb Crawford, in the qualifying round of this meeting, achieved what probably stands today as a world record—he did two holes-in-one in the same round, and finished with a score of 101.

Soon after the Birmingham tournament Bobby squared off with Perry Adair for the spectacular beating Perry had given him at Montgomery earlier in the season, and won his third invitation event of the year, at their home course, East Lake, beating Perry in the finals. It rained all through the week, and Bobby, still with ideas concerning golf ballistics, used a small ball against the wind and a big ball with the wind, in spite of which he played very good golf.

And after that came the first Georgia state amateur championship, at the Brookhaven course of the Capital City Club, Atlanta—and it was

there that Bobby, never in the least suspecting
such a thing as he entered the fray, won the spurs
which the following month entitled him to ride
all the way to the old Merion Cricket Club, near
Philadelphia, and into his first major competition,
the national amateur championship of the United
States.

By this time the sporting writers and golfers
generally in the south had concluded that there
were two boy wonders instead of one in Dixie,
and there was an unusual degree of interest in
the first Georgia state championship ever played,
because both the Atlanta stars were entered.
There also was another youngster, from Rome,
Ga., who was gaining some renown—Simpson
Dean, later a famous college player at Princeton
and intercollegiate champion of the United States.
The stage was set at Brookhaven for a great
show, and there are old-timers today who will as-
sure you that southern golf never produced a finer
drama.

The week of play began late in July, under a
hot and brilliant sky, and Atlanta's leading contestants, duly qualified, found themselves in op-
posite brackets of the "draw" of 32 players—they
could meet in the final round, by winning all the
intervening matches. Simpson Dean was in

Bobby's bracket, and while Perry was moving steadily through the other side they came together in the semi-final bout of their section. Bobby was going at a fast clip, despite some eccentricities in his driving—he was over the lumbago now and was banging the ball with all his might—and it looked as if he was a certain winner when he had the tall Roman dormie 5; that is, 5 down with only five holes to play.

There Simpson started a rally that, as Bobby confessed later, fairly rattled his teeth. He won the next three holes in succession, and at the seventeenth green had a five-foot putt to win that hole also, when the psychological effect of his spurt very likely would have carried him to an extra-hole victory; it is that way in tournament golf. But the ball, struck perfectly along the line, stopped just one turn short of the cup.

"If it had only been a yard past!" Simpson lamented, good-naturedly, as they shook hands. "But to stop *short* . . . !"

So Bobby went into the final round, in the 36-hole encounter that was to make a lot of history.

Next day the papers called it a classic struggle. I wrote one of the accounts, myself, and I know I used that term, along with a number of others, none of which (I reflected sadly) conveyed any adequate idea of what a battle it was. Bobby now was larger and stronger than Perry, though three years younger; there was little to choose in their shots, and I am sure no two golfers ever met who were better matched in courage and determination.

Bobby displayed greater power, but Perry's superior accuracy in the morning round brought him in 3 up for the luncheon intermission. Bobby's putting had betrayed him grievously at a number of greens, and after a sandwich and a glass of milk he went out to the eighteenth green to practice until time for the second round to start.

From this episode there came a story of the match, essentially a good story as told of a determined youngster, the only drawback being that it was not at all true. It was said that Ralph Reed, chairman of the tournament committee, went out to watch Bobby putting, and told him a lot of spectators had just arrived to see the afternoon round. And (the story went) he asked Bobby to "play out the bye-holes"—the holes remaining after a match ends; inferentially, after Perry, then leading 3 up, had beaten him.

"Don't worry," Bobby was said to have told Mr. Reed. "There won't be any bye-holes!"

In a way, it seems rather a pity that the story

isn't true, because the prediction certainly came true enough.

Starting the afternoon round 3 down, Bobby pulled his drive far off the fairway, shoved his second shot into the woods across the course and nearly into a lake, and lost the first hole, thus becoming 4 down, with a dismally approximated 6 at that hole. And with that calamitous start he buckled down to shoot a level 70, including the 6.

He got back one hole with a birdie 3 at the third, they halved the next three holes in par figures, and Bobby picked up the long seventh with a birdie 4.

He was now back on par again, and was only 2 down. But Bobby was under a strain of which he had never been conscious before. And I have always considered that the match turned at the eighth hole.

This was an interesting sort of mongrel affair, the drive from a tall tee across an inlet of the lake, and the green, very small and dangerously guarded, at a distance that might be covered by a big shot. Both drives, indeed, were close to the green, and after the tiny second shots both balls were within moderate holing range, Perry's four feet from the flag, Bobby's slightly farther away. The pressure now showed up clearly—and fatally, to Perry's chances. Bobby missed his putt for a 3. And then, with the chance to go 3 up again, and in all likelihood to settle the match, Perry also missed. It was a half in 4; Bobby was still 2 down, and Perry's mistake at the tenth hole finally afforded his opponent the opening he needed and with par the rest of the way Bobby won at the last green, 2 up, and was Georgia's first amateur champion in golf.

As I suggested, that match made history. For one thing, it rearranged the order in which golfers were wont to mention the favorite sons of Dixie. Up to this match it always was Perry and Bob. After that classic struggle at Brookhaven it became Bob and Perry.

And after the Georgia championship Mr. Reed insisted, to Big Bob, that Bobby had earned the right to play in the national amateur, at Merion.

"I don't know," said Big Bob, solemnly. "He's mighty young!"

And then George Adair said: "I'm taking Perry. You let Bobby come along with us!"

So Big Bob nodded.

And that is the kind of rivalry and friendship that was between those two great sportsmen who were the fathers of Bob and Perry.

CHAPTER VI

THE BIG SHOW

THERE are four major golfing championships
in which the masculine amateur is eligible to
compete—the amateur and the open championships of the United States, commonly called the
American championships, and the amateur and
open championships of Great Britain. Of these,
the open competitions are, of course, the more
important; as the term implies, they are open to
amateurs and professionals alike, not only of
Great Britain and America, but also of any other
country; they are open to the world. Amateurs,
of course, are not eligible to play in national professional championships, which also are restricted
to entries from the nation in which the competition is held, while the national amateur championships are open to any amateur competitor in the
world with a suitable ranking. This explains the
frequent presence of formidable groups of British

amateurs in our national competitions, and of American invasions of Britain. Our national amateur title has been held once by a Briton, Harold Hilton, who won it in 1911, while the British amateur crown has been worn by three Americans—the late Walter J. Travis, in 1904; Jess Sweetser, in 1926; and Bobby Jones, in 1930. Mr. Travis, it should be explained, was a naturalized citizen of the United States, born in Australia; but his victory always is regarded as an American conquest.

The cups emblematic of the British and American open championships have crossed the big pond more frequently—usually coming this way. Harry Vardon and Edward Ray, English professionals, have won our championship, Vardon in 1900 and Ray in 1920; while Jock Hutchison, Jim Barnes and Tommy Armour, transplanted from Britain to the United States, have won the British open once each, and Walter Hagen, native American professional, and Bobby Jones, Georgia amateur, have captured the little silver pitcher seven times between them in the nine years ending with 1930, Hagen's count being four and Bobby's three.

This, then, is a sort of picture of the Big Show in which Bobby made his début in the

American amateur championship of 1916 at the age of fourteen years and six months, the youngest competitor who had, through 1930, entered and qualified in the amateur classic.

Now a little picture of Bobby himself as he went to Merion.

The spindling youngster of seven, reaching twice that age, had grown into a powerful, chunky, somewhat knock-kneed boy, five feet four inches tall, weighing 165 pounds; blue-eyed, rather tow-headed; wearing long pants—he carried only one golfing pair with him to the tournament, and one pair of golf shoes, his wardrobe being of the simplest and his mind untroubled with apprehensions of rain—and regarding the expedition as the grandest lark of his life thus far. He had read and heard about the famous golfers who were to play in the tournament— Bob Gardner, then champion; Chick Evans, who had lately won the national open championship at Minneapolis, and the others; but he never had seen any of them, and he was not in the least afraid of a golfing encounter with them. In a word, he was a husky kid with a state championship under his belt, a great swing, and not enough sense or experience to fear anybody, in golf. As for the national amateur championship, that, to

Bobby, was just another golf tournament, bigger and better and farther from home than those in which he had played—but just another tournament. He had yet to learn that there is all the difference in the world between the Big Show, in any of its phases, and anything else in golf.

He learned a lot about that, in this tournament.

Mr. Adair and Perry and Bobby stayed at the Bellevue-Stratford Hotel in Philadelphia, the finest hotel Bobby had ever seen, and traveled to and from the club on suburban trains. Their first practice was on the West Course—there are two courses at the Merion Cricket Club, the tournament being played on the East Course—and the first thing that impressed him was the beautiful, smooth texture of the putting surfaces. Until he got to Merion, Bobby never had seen anything but the comparatively coarse and harsh Bermuda greens of southern courses, which, by contrast, made the Merion surfaces resemble billiard tables. And the change in speed was bewildering to the youngster, accustomed to rapping the ball firmly and decisively over the slower Bermuda.

His first experience on these new greens included a most embarrassing episode. The sixth hole of the West Course was a short pitch to the green over a brook, the slope facing the player.

Bobby's ball was some thirty feet beyond the hole, which was in the middle of the green. Forgetting for the moment all about the faster pace of the Merion surfaces, Bobby struck his putt firmly with the little center-shafted Travis putter he used in those days, and was horrified to see the ball roll past the hole, and, apparently gathering momentum, trickle right on to the other edge of the green and into the brook, so that he had to drop out on the farther bank with a penalty stroke and play 4 from there, after reaching the green with his first shot.

Our national amateur championship opened then, as now, with a qualifying round of 36 holes, the scores to determine the 32 competitors to engage in subsequent match-play. The field being too numerous for all the entrants to play two rounds of 18 holes on the same course in one day, half the competitors played one round on each of the two courses, changing over for their second round. Bobby was assigned to the West Course in the morning. It was somewhat easier than the East Course, and at the end of the first round for all competitors it was suddenly discovered that his card of 74 was best in the entire field. Word got about that the new kid from Dixie was breaking up the tournament, and when Bobby appeared to start his afternoon round, on the East Course, almost all the spectators had assembled at the first tee to watch him, in by far the largest gallery Bobby had ever seen.

Now came the first lesson in the Big Show— the gallery, always a factor and often a terrific hazard in major championship play. Always the gallery follows a favored star, a leading contender, or a new phenomenon—as in this instance. Tempered by tournament fire, the experienced competitor is less handicapped by his own gallery than are the unfortunate players immediately before and behind him, who suffer immeasurably at times from the thundering herd, as one writer has called it, rushing about in the effort to watch the performance of some one else.

This first gallery at Merion was watching Bobby, and behaving in a very orderly and proper fashion. But the concentrated stare of so many eyes, all focused on himself, afflicted the green youngster with stage-fright, a ghastly and palpitant misery to which he was a perfect stranger; his fine, powerful swing and his smooth putting-touch suddenly and hopelessly tightened up; his shots strayed hither and yon; short putts declined to drop; and to his exemplary 74 of the morning he added a terrible 89 in the afternoon.

The total of 163, however, was easily good enough to place Bobby in the charmed circle of the championship, for the highest score to qualify was 167. Perry Adair was tied at that figure with several other competitors, who had to play off the tie. He won a place among the 32 qualifiers, won his first match, and lost in the second round.

After the draw, Bobby found himself matched with Eben Byers, a former national champion, for the first round. Up to this time he never had heard of Mr. Byers, but members of the southern party at once enlightened him. Mr. Byers, they said, was a tough customer, a veteran of many campaigns. It was hard luck, they told Bobby, catching him right at the start.

Mr. Adair, however, clapped Bobby hard on the back and told him not to worry.

"Remember what old Bob Fitzsimmons used to say," he advised. "'The bigger they are, the harder they fall.'"

Bobby considered that a corking line; but anyway he was not conscious of any particular anxiety; except for the gallery—and he suspected that after his 89 there wouldn't be much of a gallery—it was just another golf match, and he went to the first tee the following morning in a frame of mind that caused him, before the match was a minute old, to encounter what he regarded at the time as a rebuff, about which he has chuckled a good many times since.

As Mr. Byers and Bobby walked off the tee after their drives, Bobby, in the same spirit as he would have done it in a casual match at home, offered the former champion a piece of chewing-gum.

Mr. Byers declined—without thanks. And Bobby, whose motive was entirely hospitable, felt somewhat abashed. This seemed to be a new way to play golf. He also wondered why Mr. Byers did not chew gum.

But he soon began to feel quite at home. Despite the absence of a big gallery he was playing badly, and he had plenty to think about, with a 36-hole match on his hands. Mr. Byers also was playing badly, and they had an exciting time. They missed shots frequently, and, though Mr. Byers was one of the oldest contestants and Bobby the youngest in the field, they expressed their feelings in precisely the same way. With the perfectly natural reactions carried over from early childhood, Bobby followed a badly missed stroke by throwing the club after the ball as far as he could. Mr. Byers did the same thing. Players in the match directly behind them said later that it looked like a juggling act on the stage. At the twelfth hole Mr. Byers hurled a club over a hedge and out of the golf course, and would not allow his caddy to go after it. This caused Bobby to explain whimsically later that he had defeated his opponent because Mr. Byers ran out of clubs first.

Displays of temperament such as this—temper probably is the better word—gained for Bobby in the next two years a good deal of adverse criticism in the newspapers, though he was by no means the only offender against golfing manners before a gallery. The sports writers loved to depict him as a "hot-blooded southerner," long after he had taken their criticisms to heart and had mastered his emotions, so far as any outward symptoms were concerned; a conquest which will be considered later, as an important part of his development in golf and otherwise.

At any rate, unhampered in this match by any thought of what the historians might say about his deportment, Bobby finally defeated the former champion 3-1, at the thirty-fifth green, and he was not at all elated by his first success in a national championship.

"I didn't deserve to win," he said. "I played rotten golf."

Which, of course, was a proper way of looking

at it. Still, he had won, and he was in the remaining sixteen who played next day in the second round, Bobby this time paired with Frank Dyer, a capable golfer in the east and a state and district champion. And here Bobby produced some really fine golf, probably the best spin of the entire tournament, so far as scoring is concerned.

Dyer started fast against his schoolboy opponent, winning five of the first six holes; the critics in the gallery shook their heads; the kid was too good to be true, they said; now he was on the run. But just here the Georgia boy displayed a faculty that was to be the determining factor in later years on many a hard-fought field—the ability to take a staggering sock on the chin and come back for more; the ability, in the slang of the game, to stand the gaff.

Where a golfer of lesser courage and heart would have folded up—would have taken the rest of the match, as the experts were saying, "on the run"—Bobby buckled down and reeled off the next twenty-eight holes in better than an average of 4's; better than the figures of Old Man Par himself. He set a pace that Dyer, even with his great lead and greater experience, could not stand. And he won the match 4-2, with the finest stretch of golf the 1916 championship produced.

THE BOYS' LIFE OF BOBBY JONES

And that was a match he could be proud of. The difference was, he had *won* this one; he felt that his opponent had *lost* the first one.

This victory revived the interest of the gallery in the Georgia boy, also that of the golf-writers, who paid him a lot of attention in the papers and wrote things which caused him to feel extremely foolish. They said things about his dusty pants and his worn shoes and his fresh young face and other personal attributes which he considered embarrassing. Bobby never had thought much about his shoes or his pants, as long as they held together. Golf was not a dress-up game, for him. And these were the only golfing togs he had brought with him. He never had thought much about his face, either, and it seemed in a way indelicate to expose it in the public prints, to say nothing of his pants. And the galleries, the largest he had ever seen, contained only a half-dozen familiar faces. But he found everybody curiously friendly, and he got the idea then and there that "these Yankees" must be pretty good folks, after all.

He had got over his stage-fright before a big gallery, too, having gone through his baptism of fire; and it was a huge gallery that watched him and his opponent in the next round, for here, with the field now reduced to eight, he met Robert A. Gardner of Chicago, the amateur champion, in a battle which was to have a very definite effect on Bobby's golfing education.

For more than two-thirds of that bout Bobby held his own, and rather outplayed Gardner, who was working under the handicap of an infected finger, his longer shots tending to wildness in consequence. Bobby did a 76 in the morning round and was 1 up. The afternoon round found them still playing evenly, the match being square as they went to the sixth tee. And here the tournament lesson began.

Bobby was hitting his shots with great accuracy, and when he planted his second on the sixth green, five yards from the flag, he felt certain of going into the lead once more, as Gardner's second missed the green on the right, in a difficult place from which to approach with his third. But he chipped stone dead for his par 4, and got a half.

The next hole was almost a repetition. Bobby's second shot was five yards below the cup, and Gardner missed the green by several yards, on the left. But again the champion chipped dead for a half.

Still, the Georgia schoolboy wasn't discouraged. "He can't keep on missing shots and getting away with it," Bobby reflected. "He can't chip dead all the time. I'll get him yet!"

At the eighth hole, a drive and a short pitch, Bobby's second shot was only ten feet from the pin, and Gardner's pitch sent his ball clear over on to the ninth tee—and this time he didn't chip dead; his third left the ball a dozen feet from the hole, farther away in three shots than Bobby was in two.

"And now" (thought Bobby) "I've got him! I thought he couldn't keep on doing it!"

And then—well, then Gardner sank his 12-foot putt, and Bobby missed his 10-footer. And it was another half.

It seemed he *could* keep on doing it.

Ten years later it might have been a different story. Ten years later Bobby had learned the lesson he was starting to learn then—that the iron pressure of par golf must break through the most spectacular procession of brilliant recoveries. Ten years later Bobby had learned to keep the pressure on, even when an opponent's run of breaks seemed endless.

But this was not ten years later. This was in Bobby's first appearance in the Big Show, at Merion, in 1916. And here he had kept the iron pressure of Old Man Par on Bob Gardner as long as he could—and it was not Gardner who broke. It was Bobby. He lost five of the next seven holes. Gardner beat him 5-3, holing a 20-foot putt for a par 4 at the fifteenth, after driving out of bounds.

Next day, a well-written account of the match contained this paragraph:

Carefree and unconcerned, save with the big dish of ice-cream awaiting him at the clubhouse, the Georgia schoolboy swung along from the fifteenth green in his worn shoes and dusty pants and sweat-streaked shirt, whistling an air from a recent musical comedy, as jaunty and complacent as if he had just won his first national championship instead of having been beaten in the third round. He was thinking about the ice-cream.

But he wasn't. Early in life, early in his golfing career, Bobby learned to face defeat with a smile and to take a licking as a sportsman should.

But he wasn't thinking about the ice-cream as he swung along from the fifteenth green toward the clubhouse. He was thinking about that match.

Long afterward Bobby told me he never had learned anything from a match that he had won.

"I've learned what I know from beatings," he said.

He was learning something about the Big Show, now.

CHAPTER VII

PLAYING FOR THE RED CROSS

SO BOBBY JONES was defeated in the third match of his first national championship, but in less than a week the Georgia schoolboy had become famous; more famous than he realized at the time. At fourteen he became the outstanding youngster in the world of golf. And in a way this was a difficult situation. Never again did he present himself at a major championship unheralded. The fierce glare of the spotlight was upon him as he went to the first tee of the first round; he was the pet of the galleries and the golf-writers alike. He was accorded a good chance of winning every competition in which he took part; he was ranked higher and higher in the list of favorites; and through seven years, beginning at Merion in 1916, he played in ten major championships—without winning one. These "seven lean years," as they have been called, constitute a chapter in the history of a world champion which very likely is without a counterpart in any sport; certainly in golf. Seven years of unvaried defeat in the Big Show, and all the time regarded as one of its leading performers, would have broken the heart of any but a champion. The "seven fat years" which came later, reversing the Scriptural order, bore no finer testimony of a real champion who first of all was able to stand the gaff.

And of course, after his match with Bob Gardner, Bobby was back at the Merion Club next day and the day after that, with Mr. Adair and Perry, watching the last two matches of the 1916 amateur championship—watching his conqueror defeat Jesse Guilford, the Boston Siege Gun— longest driver of the American amateur ranks— while Chick Evans, the open champion, was winning his way past Clarke Corkran, to match shots on Saturday with Gardner. He watched that match with an almost hypnotic interest; it was as if he realized subconsciously that here were two great golfers with whom he had many a hand to play in the future; and he saw Evans, defeating the Chicagoan 4-3, add the amateur title to the open championship and become the first double champion of the United States, and the only one, until Bobby did it himself, fourteen years later.

Incidentally, Bobby missed a putting-lesson that week which might very well have changed the course of events for him in the next seven years.

Attending the tournament was the late Walter J. Travis, who had won the American amateur championship three times, in 1900, 1901, and 1903, and the British title in 1904; a remarkable golfer who took up the game at thirty-five and reached its front rank by accuracy and intelligence—and the deadliest putting-stroke of his generation. It was his cold concentration and machine-like precision on the greens that caused a somewhat grudging British admirer, watching him in the final match of the latter championship, to say of him:

"If you stuck a knife in that man, he'd bleed ice-water!"

Mr. Travis took a great interest in Bobby's performance at Merion. When asked by a golf-writer what he thought of Bobby's prospects in the way of improvement, Mr. Travis replied, bluntly:

"Improvement? He can never improve his shots, if that's what you mean. But he will learn a great deal more about playing them. And his putting method is faulty."

And the Grand Old Man, as he was called, invited Bobby to come out half an hour before the matches were to start next morning, and have a little lesson in that vastly important art.

But Mr. Adair and his party missed the earlier train and Bobby arrived at the time the matches were starting. And Mr. Travis, always a stickler for punctuality, went out with the gallery, and the chance for the lesson was lost.

At any rate, it was postponed nearly eight years—and that also is an interesting bit of history.

In the early spring of 1924, Bobby, then a woefully erratic putter, though he had won the American open championship the previous summer, played with Perry Adair an exhibition match at Augusta, Ga., against Arthur Havers and James Ockenden, then open champions of Great Britain and France, respectively. Mr. Travis was in the gallery and saw Bobby do some putting which was even worse than usual, while he and Perry took a fine lacing from the professionals. And after the match, in the locker-room of the Augusta Country Club, I was privileged to be present when Mr. Travis gave Bobby that long-deferred lesson, in the guise of a lecture, which so changed his putting in a single season that from one of the worst performers among the champions, he became one of the finest and most consistent putters the game has seen.

There may be a place farther along to explain just what Mr. Travis told Bobby in that belated lesson; and certainly it is interesting to speculate on what effect the same lecture in 1916 might have had on the seven lean years. However, that opportunity was lost; and, anyway, Bobby might have been too young and too green to profit by it, as he did after he had been through the mill. A lost opportunity sometimes does return, in spite of Senator Ingall's fine sonnet—and perhaps it returns at a better time.

So that was all of golf for the eventful year 1916, and the next spring our country got into the Big War, and there were no national championships played in 1917 or 1918, though the southern amateur event was held, and Bobby won it, over the same course at the Roebuck Country Club of Birmingham, where he captured his first important invitation tournament two years before. His experience in the national championship had given him poise and confidence; he played with dash and precision, and he went steadily through the five matches, defeating Reuben Bush of New Orleans, the south's leading stylist, in the semi-finals, and Louis Jacoby of the same city, later of

Dallas, in the last round after a lapse which would
have illustrated with great clarity, had Bobby only
been wise enough to see it, the importance of care
in the matter of diet during a hard golf competition. At the end of the morning round Bobby
was 4 up—a fine, comfortable lead. At luncheon
he was in high good humor, and hungry, with
the healthy appetite of a growing boy. In place
of the tea and toast which later became his standard repast—if indeed he ate anything at all between rounds—he treated himself liberally to pie
and ice-cream, went out on the first tee for the
afternoon round in a state of mind and body as
far removed as possible from keenness, and lost
the first three holes to his more experienced adversary. The shock of these successive mishaps,
and perhaps the processes of digestion, restored
him to something like the proper attitude; from
the fourth tee he stuck a full iron shot of 200
yards three inches from the hole, won it, and went
on to win the match and the championship, 6-5.

The western amateur championship also was
played this year, and Bobby made a valiant effort
to add that title to the southern—he and three
other Atlanta boys all qualified in the tournament,
at Chicago, and all were beaten in the first round,

Bobby losing to Ned Sawyer. Francis Ouimet of Boston won the title.

Soon after this tournament Mr. J. A. Scott of the Wright & Ditson Company arranged a tour of exhibition golf matches for the war chest of the American Red Cross, inviting four young players to take part—those inseparable friends, Bob and Perry of Atlanta; Alexa Stirling of the same city and Elaine Rosenthal of Chicago, two of the best of the feminine golfers of America. Miss Stirling had won her first of three national championships in the early fall of 1916 at Boston, soon after Bobby had played in the masculine amateur championship at Merion. Mrs. Rosenthal chaperoned the party, and the youngsters had a wonderful trip, or, rather, series of trips. They played at Boston and New London and Holyoke and Ekwanok, and at Maplewood, up in New Hampshire, and Poland Spring, and Essex— dozens of interesting places—Bobby paired with Alexa one day and with Elaine the next. Later, Bob and Perry played in similar matches against famous amateurs: Chick Evans and Bob Gardner at Chicago and Kansas City, the veterans trouncing the kids in good battles, while at St. Louis the Atlanta boys finally won a great match against Chick and the late Warren K. Wood.

They played other matches in Dallas and Houston and Fort Worth, where Bobby shot a 70 and broke the course record; and then at Galveston and then home, where, on July 4, 1918, I saw them in a match against Jimmy Standish and Kenneth Edwards, winning by a narrow margin in a round of which I saw only the start and the finish; I was convalescing on crutches from a severe illness which had got into an old football injury in my left knee and wrecked it beyond repair; from that time on I traveled about golf courses with a stiff leg, which, you may be sure, is no great help when coping with a gallery of fifteen or twenty thousand pop-eyed spectators giving an accurate imitation of the thundering herd.

I remember particularly that Bob and Perry wore bright-red Swiss Guard caps somebody had given them in St. Louis; they wore them in all their matches thereafter, until they were lost, and very brilliant and showy I thought they looked. I remember, too, that Forrest Adair auctioned off the four positions as caddies to prominent club members, who paid several hundred dollars each for the privilege of lugging heavy bags of clubs around a long course on a very warm after-

noon—the money, of course, going to the Red
Cross fund along with the gate receipts.

Soon after that Bobby received a telegram
from Chick Evans that Warren Wood, who was
to have toured the east with Chick for the Red
Cross, was ill and asking Bobby to take his place,
and the champion and Bobby played a fine match
with two professionals, Jack Dowling and Tom
McNamara, at a New York club, Scarsdale, and
were beaten by a single hole. They met the same
pair again over the North Shore course and lost,
2 up. Chick and Bobby individually played about
as well as the pros, but the latter teamed better—
a great factor in what is known as four-ball competition, where the best score of each side counts
at each hole.

And then came the historic War Relief matches
at three eastern courses, in which Bobby found
himself pitted against professional players in real
earnest for the first time, and discovered that
the amateurs might learn a lot from such competition. He had never engaged in a tournament
with professionals up to that time, but in these
encounters he discovered also a great liking for
competition with them, and throughout the latter part of his career I believe he preferred the
open championships to the amateur events.

The War Relief matches were arranged in a singularly interesting fashion. Four teams were chosen—Amateurs, Homebred Professionals, Scottish Professionals, and English Professionals; and all encountered each of the others in foursomes and singles matches, the former, of course, being in the traditional Scottish mode, in which the two partners play alternate strokes with the same ball, the only true type of foursome.

The first match was played at the Baltusrol Golf Club, Short Hills, N. J., and the Amateurs had a rather distressing time of it. In the foursomes, played in the morning, they met the English Professionals while the Homebreds fought it out with the Scottish Pros. Bobby was paired with Norman Maxwell against George Sargent and Herbert Strong, and they were the only Amateurs to count for their side. In the afternoon, they did somewhat better at singles. Several of them won points, Bobby in particular beating Cyril Walker 1 up after Walker started by taking the first three holes. He got into a frame of mind aptly described by Robert Louis Stevenson in the duel scene in *The Master of Ballantrae* as "a contained and glowing fury." He did not throw any clubs away, but he did the next six holes 4-3-4-4-4-2, winning five of them and turning 2

91

up. His humor cooled somewhat, coming in, but he managed to hold a small lead.

The other two matches were played at Siwanoy, a New York course, and Garden City, Long Island, the famous design of Walter J. Travis— narrow and perilous to the long, wild hitter, and, Mr. Travis's critics always asserted, laid out to suit his own short but desperately accurate game. It was on this course that Bobby and Perry Adair, paired in the foursomes, played the worst match of their association; they were both wild. Bobby would follow a good drive by Perry with a scandalous hook into the deep rough, or, if Perry happened to drive off the fairway, Bobby would spank the ball clear across into trouble on the other side. They were playing Jack Dowling and Emmett French, who were steady and conservative and won easily, 8-7.

In all, however, Bobby did pretty well in this series of brushes with the professionals. He played three matches at singles and was the only member of the Amateur side who escaped a defeat. And in another exhibition bout, just before the War Relief events, he stumbled on a bit of psychology which he pondered a good deal afterward, with some profit.

He and Perry were playing Jack Hobens and

Nipper Campbell, professionals, in a 36-hole medal competition at Englewood, N. J., in which the total score was to count for each player. Bobby started with a 3 at the first hole and another 3 at the second—both par 4 holes. As they walked toward the next tee Jack said to him, casually:

"Well, Bobby, eighteen 3's make 54, you know!"

And Bobby was shocked by his subsequent performance. He hit scarcely another decent shot, and finished the round with a depressing 80. As he reasoned it out—later—he began thinking about making 3's, and not about Old Man Par, and as a result he was doing frequent 5's and an occasional 6 from that point onward.

In other bouts, Chick Evans and Bobby defeated Jerry Travers and John Anderson, 5-3, at New Britain—Travers was the distinguished veteran who had won four amateur championships and one open, and Bobby turned in the best card of the match, a 71. He and Chick also defeated Anderson and Max Marston at Baltusrol; the summer of 1918 was the busiest of his golfing career, though no important tournaments or championships were played that year. But he gained an enormous amount of experience in competition; he enjoyed the traveling and the making of new friends and the meeting of new adversaries—and it is estimated that in the exhibition events in which he took part the American Red Cross and the War Relief funds gained more than $150,000, so Bobby's share in the Big War was not so inconsiderable, after all.

One other thing he learned, in 1918, playing before great galleries in many states. The reports of his club-throwing at Merion two years before had followed him; his temper was by way of becoming proverbial; and when he indulged occasionally in this method of blowing off steam after missing a shot inexcusably, the eastern scribes took him to task—not always too kindly, or with the reflection that, after all, this brilliant golfer was only a boy of fifteen or sixteen. They saw him play golf that any man might be proud of and that few could equal; they expected him also to present to the gallery the imperturable front of the case-hardened veteran—which, by the way, the case-hardened veteran does not always present, in times of unusual stress.

And they wrote things about him in the papers, and Bobby, in the little scrapbook he kept in the early days, was careful to paste those comments along with the more pleasant clippings. He did more than merely paste them in a book. To employ a very old and expressive bit of slang, he pasted them in his hat as well.

In that old book today you would find an occasional clipping like this one, which appeared in a Boston paper in 1918, when Bobby and Perry and Alexa Stirling and Elaine Rosenthal played a match for the Red Cross at Brae Burn:

Some interesting golf was shown during the match, interspersed with some pranks by Jones, which will have to be corrected if this player expects to rank with the best in the country. Although Jones is only a boy, his display of temper when things went wrong did not appeal to the gallery.

Whatever his "expectations" as to rank—and I am sure they were quite as modest and as vague as any boy could entertain—Bobby thought about those comments a lot, back in the bright summer of 1918, and for some time afterward. And if he still kept a scrapbook, which he does not, he might paste in it a clipping from the editorial page of the London *Times*, which contains this line:

By strength of character he has subdued a naturally fiery temper till he plays the game outwardly as a man of ice.

And long before that line was written, and not long after the criticism at Brae Burn, the gallery demeanor of Bobby Jones, even more than his beautiful game, had come to be recognized as "the glass of fashion and the mold of form."

CHAPTER VIII

BOBBY played in four championship tournaments in 1919—two sectional and two national events—without winning any, and because he finished second in three of them, that period of his career has come to be known as his "runner-up year." He was runner-up in the southern open, the Canadian open, and the United States amateur championships. At New Orleans, in the southern amateur, he was stopped in the semifinal round by Nelson Whitney, many times winner of the event, so his defense of the title he had won at its last playing, in 1917, came to a somewhat sudden conclusion.

Bobby's experience in the southern open was, in a way, a continuation of that acquired the previous year in the Red Cross and War Relief matches; again he was at grips with the professionals—it was Bobby's first open tournament, in which they competed; and certainly the southern open of 1919 was one of the liveliest and most spectacular of his career. As in so many later open championships, Bobby, at the age of seventeen, proved to be the only amateur in the field capable of matching shots with the pros, and his two-round duel with Long Jim Barnes, as they fought it out down the stretch, remains a classic chapter in the history of southern golf.

The young Georgian had been gaining inches and losing pounds since his first appearance in the Big Show three years earlier. At seventeen, he was five feet seven inches tall and weighed 150 pounds—he was three inches taller and fifteen pounds lighter than the "chunky schoolboy" at Merion. He was now in college, his first year at the Georgia School of Technology completed as the 1919 tournament season opened. The numerous bouts at golf in the last two years had given his game finish and an added consistency, and, playing on his home course, the young amateur was considered a worthy rival of the professional experts who assembled to play for a purse which was regarded as an important one in those days.

The confidence of the critics was not misplaced. At the end of the second round of the 72-hole competition, Jim Barnes was leading the field by a single stroke—and it was Bobby Jones who was running second.

As is customary in minor tournaments at medal play, the leading contenders were paired for the last two rounds; and Long Jim Barnes—he was a head taller than Bobby, and always carried a four-leaf clover in his mouth when playing golf—and the East Lake amateur set out with a fine gallery for the third round.

The first half of this round treated the gallery to one of the most amazing bursts of golf in American annals—and it was Long Jim and his four-leaf clover who produced most of it.

They led off with good par 4's at the first hole. Then Bobby sank a chip-shot for a 2 from the back of the second green while Jim was doing a par 3, and the score was tied—Bobby had got back the stroke by which Barnes led him as the round began. Inspired by this gain, his young nerves tingling, Bobby rammed down a 40-foot putt for a birdie 3 from the back of the third green, and felt sure he was going into the lead. But Long Jim just looked at him, changed the four-leaf clover to the other side of his mouth, inspected the line of his own putt—it was at least 30 feet—and canned the ball for a 3 also.

This started the fireworks. Bobby played the

first six holes of that round 2 strokes better than par—and lost 3 strokes! Against a par of 4-3-4-5-5-3 Long Jim Barnes traveled 4-3-3-4-3-2. Bobby played the fourth, fifth, and sixth holes in absolute par—and lost four strokes on those holes! Barnes was producing golf of the super-brilliant type which couples fine play with good fortune; and even Old Man Par himself cannot hold the pace, while it lasts.

The long fifth hole was the back-breaker for Bobby, and, as things turned out, it probably was the hole which decided the championship.

The fifth hole at East Lake, at tournament stretch, was 620 yards in length, one of the longest holes in the world. In front of the green was a low mound and a bunker, which concealed most of the surface from a player more than a hundred yards away, the flag, however, being in plain view.

Here it looked as if Bobby might get a stroke back from the flying Barnes, for his drive was straight down the fairway and his second shot just over a hundred yards from the green, while Barnes pulled his drive to the rough at the left and then shoved his brassie far across the fairway to the rough at the other side, 150 yards from the flag.

Long Jim played a mashie pitch. The ball sailed over the mound and the bunker and descended lightly on the green. There was a moment's pause, and then a roar from the gallery back of the green. The ball had bounded once, skidded as the backspin took hold, and then trickled straight to the pin and dropped into the hole! It was an eagle 3.

And Bobby's neat par 5 was good only for the loss of two strokes there. And Long Jim, still inspired, shot a deuce at him on the short Island Hole, picking up another stroke against Bobby's par 3. That gave Barnes a lead of four strokes. At the end of the morning's play he was six strokes ahead of the young amateur, with one more round to go.

Bobby kept after the tall Cornishman persistently, but did not gain a stroke in the first nine holes that afternoon. Then Long Jim, a bit careless in choosing his stance on the tenth tee, planted his right foot on some loose turf, slipped ever so little as he brought the club on the ball, and topped it into the lake. Bobby with a par 4 got back two strokes there, and collected two more by the time they reached the last hole, of 210 yards. Here Barnes played cautiously, taking two putts from a distance of four feet, and Bobby's par 3 pulled him up to within a single stroke. But Long Jim Barnes was the first southern open champion, and Bobby was runner-up.

When he went to New Orleans, Bobby was the hold-over champion of the Southern Golf Association. He had won the title at Birmingham in 1917, and the tournament was not held in 1918, due to the war. And he and Nelson Whitney, playing on his home course, were the co-favorites in the 1919 event. With the Atlanta contingent at least Bobby was the leading favorite. He had won handily two years before, he was a better golfer now, and it was expected that the added experience would count heavily, even against Whitney —who, by the way, had not played in the 1917 championship.

His very first shot of the competition, however, showed that however much Bobby's preceding two years had improved his golf, there was something left for him to learn about the rules.

The incident now is one of the classic anecdotes of golf. It has been told many times, often inaccurately, and perhaps it is as well for me, as an eye-witness, to set it down here as it really happened.

At that time the first hole of the New Orleans Country Club course was a one-shotter of 150 yards. Bobby's mashie pitch from the tee was pulled off to the left of the green, and the ball landed in a wheelbarrow, left there by some workman. Worse than that, it landed in an old shoe, beside which the wheelbarrow contained another shoe, a lawnmower, some greasy rags, and a quantity of cut grass.

The rule on "upkeep" applies, of course. A player in this or a similar situation is entitled to lift the ball and drop it, not nearer the hole, without penalty, the wheelbarrow not being part of the golf course.

But Bobby did not know the rule; at any rate, he was not sure of its provisions, and he was taking no chances of disqualification in the medal round that determined the qualifiers for the championship.

He studied the situation, which appeared remarkably gloomy. The only ray of light was the condition of the shoe, which was an old one and did not look as if it would hold together long under a determined attack with a niblick. And, indeed, Bobby did take a niblick finally, planted himself as firmly as possible on the ground beside the wheelbarrow, and walloped the shoe as hard as he could. To his immense relief, the shoe was projected to the green, where the ball rolled out, and he got it down in two putts for a 4, losing a stroke to par.

And the moral to that is—learn the rules!

Bobby qualified easily and safely, but had he not been playing well that stroke might have left him out of the championship. He studied the rules, after that, and thereafter I cannot recall a single predicament of his career in which he did not know exactly what the rules permitted and did not permit.

Nelson Whitney was in the same bracket with Bobby and they met in the semi-final round. In the morning play there was little to choose; they were as evenly matched as possible. But in the afternoon Bobby, starting out with the match all square, went after his opponent with his original idea of match-play—to win as quickly as possible, instead of keeping the pressure on, as Whitney was doing. Trying too hard, he began missing a shot here and there, and the New Orleans veteran, playing coolly and steadily, allowed Bobby to beat himself by his own mistakes—as he did, very conclusively, by a margin of 6-5. The Atlanta delegation was heart-broken; Bobby began to perceive vaguely that there was more than one way of playing a golf match; and Whitney went on to defeat Jacoby in the finals next day.

The Canadian open championship of 1919 was what might be called a one-man show, and the man was the late J. Douglas Edgar, a little English professional who had come over to the Druid Hills Golf Club of Atlanta early that spring. He and Bobby, with Perry Adair and Willie Ogg, then professional at East Lake—Stewart Maiden had gone for a time to the St. Louis Country Club—played many matches in Atlanta, and Bobby had little difficulty holding his own, or a bit more, with the Englishman. Edgar was the most temperamental of golfers. When in the mood—when he felt "right"—he could play incredibly beautiful golf; when he did not feel right, he simply declined to bear down, as the saying is, and he played in a very ordinary manner, considering his ability. His style was individual and somewhat unorthodox, in that he kept the club hooded, or with its face turned as much as possible toward the ball, during the stroke.

The story of the Canadian open at Hamilton, Ontario, was that Douglas Edgar felt right. Bobby went to that tournament playing very good golf, and he played very good golf all through it, winding up in a tie with the same Long Jim Barnes who beat him by a single stroke in the southern open, and Karl Keffer, Canadian professional. Their score for the 72 holes was 294, which is an excellent figure in a national open championship.

But they were tied for *second place*. And they were *sixteen* strokes back of the amazing Englishman. Edgar's cards, in the order of their performance, were 72-71-69-66, for a total of 278, a score which remained for years the lowest ever returned in a national competition in any country. And Edgar's performance at Hamilton remains to this day the most conclusive drubbing ever administered to a crack field of contestants in an important open championship.

Bobby came to the last green with two putts to be the runner-up all by himself—and he took three! Still, he was undeniably runner-up—with two companions.

And the last tournament of the year saw Bobby again in the Big Show, his second appearance in the United States amateur championship, at the great course of the Oakmont Country Club, Pittsburgh. In spite of the fact that he had not won any titles that season, Bobby's showing had been so good, especially in the Southern and Canadian open events, against the professionals, that when he went to Oakmont he was regarded as having nearly as good a chance as the great rivals, Chick Evans, who had won the last American amateur, at Merion, and Francis Ouimet. Bobby, however, had not been satisfied with his driving all season, and Big Bob was even less pleased with it. So when the date of the championship drew near and Bobby continued strewing his big shots all over the place, Big Bob sent him out to St. Louis, for his first model and mentor, Stewart Maiden, to straighten him out. And for the first and, I think, the only time in Bobby's career, Stewart seemed unable to help him. After a couple of days of unmitigated and unsuccessful toil at St. Louis, Stewart decided to go on with Bobby to the championship, and Big Bob joined them there.

The Oakmont course was, and is, a tremendous test of golf, and the first qualifying round was complicated further by a severe hailstorm. So all the scores ran high, all the way up to 172, which was the worst score to qualify. In spite of erratic driving, Bobby worked around to a total of 159 and was next to Jimmy Manion and Paul Tewkesbury, who shared the medalist's position with 158—and these were the only scores under 160, or an average of 80 for each of the two rounds.

At Oakmont, Bobby's driving had failed to improve. He was trying to "steer" the shots, as it is called—one of the least possible things in golf —and Stewart's final advice to him, after an unhappy session on a practice tee, was to go out there and hit the ball as hard as he could and forget all about staying in the fairway.

"If you get off the course," said the Silent Scot, sagely, "you'll be nearer to the green, anyway!"

Also, at Oakmont, it is possible for a very long hitter who is badly off the line to send the ball clear over the guarding bunkers at the side of the fairway and find no great trouble for his next shot.

Sticking to this simple plan and walloping the ball with all his might, Bobby defeated Jimmy Manion in the first round and in his next match, with Bob Gardner, who had beat him at Merion three years before, he played the first nine holes in 35, a stroke better than par, with most of his drives finding the rough. He was 3 up at the turn and went on to win rather easily, 5-4. It was in this round that the match occurred which sent the two leading favorites out of the picture. Evans and Ouimet came together, neither of them in the best physical condition—the hailstorm of the first qualifying round had been followed by a hard rain in the first round of the match-play, and Ouimet, the night before the match with Evans, was reported with a temperature and not far from pneumonia, while Chick was suffering from rheumatism.

In spite of this, they produced the feature match of the entire tournament, and, playing with superb courage and nerve, traveled the first 27 holes with scores that were better than par of the huge course. Bobby, whose battle with Gardner was over early, watched the closing holes in amazement—it was a battle of giants. They were square as they played the last hole; good drives were followed by second shots which left both balls bunkered; Chick blasted his way out seven feet from the pin and Francis was a foot nearer. Then Chick missed his putt and Francis sank his. Chick was out of the championship, and Francis, terribly drained by the combat, was beaten next day by Woody Platt in another grueling encounter that went to the thirty-eighth green.

And that left Bobby, who had beaten Rudolph Knepper in the third round, the pick of the critics to win.

But down in the lower bracket, with Evans and Ouimet now on the sidelines, was plugging along a large, plump, curly-haired Pittsburgh golfer with an exquisite putting-touch on the keen Oak-

mont greens—Davidson Herron, who was playing better golf than Bobby, while not so much
in the spotlight. After his first match he was
winning by big margins, and while Bobby was
defeating W. C. Fownes, Jr., 5-3, in the semi-
final round, Davy was avenging Ouimet on the
hapless Mr. Platt in the ratio of 7-6. And this
round brought Bobby to the final match of the
second national amateur in which he had played,
with the bulky Oakmont entrant as his adversary.

Herron had been playing well all week, and
Bobby seemed at last to have found his own game;
he played better than in any previous match, and
at the end of the morning round they were square.
In the afternoon, however, Davy's superior accuracy on the greens began to tell—what a difference that long-postponed putting lesson by the Old
Master, Walter Travis, might have made just
then!—and as one long putt after another from
Davy's machine-like stroke found the hole Bobby
stood on the twelfth tee 3 down.

Here was the finishing break of the battle, for,
after Davy's drive had found a bunker, with an
indifferent recovery, Bobby appeared certain to
win back a hole, perhaps to start a rally. And
here occurred an incident which, as it occupies a

prominent place in American golfing history, may properly be recounted with some detail.

The twelfth hole at Oakmont is of 600 yards; a vast affair the green of which seldom has been reached in two shots. Bobby had a great drive, and, after Herron's bunker experience, the Georgia boy was in the act of playing as big a brassie shot as possible, with a chance of reaching the green or, at the worst, of being very close to it.

As the club came to the top of the swing, a gallery official, watching the crowd and not the play, saw a distant part of the gallery in motion.

And he bellowed "Fore!" through the megaphone he carried.

In all golf there is nothing so utterly devastating to the nerves of a highly-strung player executing a shot as a sudden and unexpected sound. Compared with it motion in the gallery is nothing. The experienced competitor can protect himself against anything that assails only his vision, by simply not playing until stillness is restored. But there is no protection against unexpected sound. The reaction of the player is involuntary—and instantaneous.

Bobby flinched at the critical point of his great swing. The club hit the ball on top. The ball went hopping into a bunker. Still shaken from the experience, Bobby failed on his recovery, and gave up the hole. Where he might have been only 2 down, he was now 4 down, with six holes to play. He went on to lose, 5-4.

Bobby was runner-up. Davy Herron was champion.

It was the first really bitter disappointment Bobby had met; but it would be a grievous mistake to charge his defeat to the famous "megaphone incident," as it is called. Bobby never made that mistake. He told me not long ago that he always had been sure Davy would have beaten him, anyway—Davy was playing the better golf, he said.

One way and another, there was a great deal said and written about the "megaphone incident," and at least one very fine thing came of it.

You never see a megaphone in the gallery at a major championship nowadays.

CHAPTER IX

IN HIS competitive golfing career of fifteen
years, beginning at the age of thirteen with his
first southern amateur championship, Bobby
Jones played in forty-nine major and sectional
tournaments in which a title was at stake, not
counting club championships, invitation affairs,
and the like. Of the forty-nine, thirty-one were
major championships—national competitions of
the United States and Great Britain; one was the
Canadian open; and seventeen were regional
events, including five of the "winter loop" open
tournaments which of recent years have attracted
so many brilliant fields of professionals. Through
his "runner-up year," 1919, Bobby had played
in nine of these championships, seven minor and
two major events. Beginning with the year 1920,
then, and going through 1930, in the fall of which
year he announced his retirement from competi-

tive golf, he played in just forty championships, of which twenty-nine were of the major class. To this amazing list may be added five Walker Cup international team matches in which Bobby played with the American side against the British, the last two times as captain. And this record, compressed into eleven years and about the same number of chapters, naturally will limit our consideration to the more important features of a career which, through 1919, has been treated with a good deal of particularity.

There was an object in this. I wanted especially to set before you a well-defined background of Bobby Jones, the boy, before the "fierce white light" that plays upon a world-figure should focus your attention exclusively on Bobby Jones, the champion. I wanted you to be well acquainted with Bobby Jones, a sturdy American schoolboy, through the formative years of study and play, of light-hearted battle and bitter disappointment, which went into the making of a world champion, and—what is far more worthy—the building of a character.

Beginning with 1920, we shall be concerned almost exclusively with competitive golf in its major phases. It was in this year that Bobby first played in the United States open, which has come to be regarded as the premier golfing event of the world, though sharing that distinction nominally with the British open championship. Despite his previous appearance in two United States amateur championships, I have always regarded his début at Inverness as his real entrance on the world-stage of sport—and, happily enough, that championship was won by a great English professional, Edward Ray, while Harry Vardon, six times British open champion, and American champion in 1900—Harry Vardon, the Old Master, was in a quadruple tie in second place.

As the tournament season of 1920 opened, Bobby was eighteen years old. He had completed his sophomore year at Georgia Tech. and was the leading member of its golf team. He had been defeated in the semi-final round of the Georgia state championship at the Druid Hills Golf Club, Atlanta, by Veazy Rainwater, who went on to win the title from Tom Prescott, another member of the Tech. team; but had captured the southern amateur championship in brilliant fashion at Chattanooga, his last two completed rounds in that tournament being 70 and 69. His performance was so impressive that two Atlanta sportsmen, Lowry Arnold and Tom Paine, urged his entry, with several other southern boys, in the western amateur championship, played at Memphis the following week, with Chick Evans of Chicago, perennial champion of the western association, in the rôle of favorite.

At Memphis Bobby started the week of play as brilliantly as he had concluded that in Chattanooga. His qualifying rounds were 69 and 70— a new record for the western—and in the first round, playing with a four-man team from the southern association, the other members being Perry Adair and Tom Prescott of Atlanta and Pollack Boyd of Chattanooga, that 69 proved the score which gave the southern team the huge Olympic Cup, which, until the first Walker Cup international match in 1922, was the largest golfing trophy Bobby had ever seen.

All the Dixie delegation felt sure that Bobby was going to win the western championship. He was more at home on the Bermuda greens than Evans, and he was playing in his very best form. But Chick, an experienced veteran, national open and amateur champion of 1916, and on his way to another national title that same year, stopped him in the semi-final round, 1 up in 36 holes, in one of the finest and most spectacular matches ever seen, just when the youngster from Atlanta seemed to hold the last trump of a winning hand.

Playing steadily and smartly, Evans worked his way to a lead of 3 up with seven holes to play. Then Bobby won back those three holes in dizzy succession, two of them by sticking approach shots dead to the flag. Though the match was square, the advantage was all with the younger player. Evans appeared to be tiring fast; and more than that, he had been hit with the hardest blow in golf—to see an apparently commanding lead cut away from under him on successive holes. But the Chicagoan continued to play his game—he declined to curl up under pressure. The next two holes were halved; and then, at the seventeenth—the thirty-fifth of the match—the Georgian seemed certain to take the lead with only one more hole to play. Evans's second shot, a big iron, was pulled to the left of the green into a deep trap with heavy grass, more puzzling than sand, at the bottom, while Bobby was on the green. Chick played a fine recovery, a dozen feet from the pin, and Bobby's long approach putt, badly struck, was half as far away. Still, with Chick's reputation as a poor putter—a reputation which I never have been able to take for granted, some way—it looked like no worse than a half for Bobby.

Then Chick sank his putt. And Bobby's ball,

touching the rim of the cup, rolled right around it and bobbed up on the other side.

That was the match, of course. A half in par 4 at the last hole ended it. . . . I think Bobby's education in competitive golf contains few better lessons than that engagement; and I know he has often said he never enjoyed a battle more.

Big Bob, back in Atlanta, lacked something of enjoying the bout, or, at least, the result. He was at the station when Bobby and I got home. He asked me several questions about the match. Then he meditated a moment. Then he said:

"Well, he'll never beat him again!"

Big Bob was referring to Chick, of course. And what he said, there at the station in Atlanta, turned out a prophecy. Chick and Bobby met twice more, in national championships, and Chick never beat him again. . . . It is a somewhat curious fact that, many times as Bobby Jones was beaten in championship competition, the same man never beat him twice. In the list are three champions who beat him once—Chick Evans and Bob Gardner and Francis Ouimet. Bobby met them all afterward, in national competition. And he beat Evans twice, and Gardner twice, and Ouimet three times. Some people affect to rate lightly the influence of heredity, but I think no one could be very close to Bobby without seeing in him, and in more evidences than that of golf, the iron spirit of Big Bob Jones.

This time, however, Chick Evans went on to win the western championship, defeating Clarence Wolff of St. Louis in the final match; and then came the southern open championship—or, rather, we will consider it next, briefly, as a sort of curtain-raiser for a more detailed account of the first national open. Douglas Edgar, the little English professional at the Druid Hills Golf Club, Atlanta, won this Southern in beautiful fashion, reminiscent of his tremendous performance the preceding season in the Canadian open. And again Bobby was runner-up, close behind him, in a fine field which included many of the leading American professionals. Edgar was in the mood; he was "right," much as he had been at Hamilton; as he used to say, his hands felt thin. And his final round was a remarkable exhibition of perfect control and fancy golf which rarely was played straight—he was bending the shots this way and that, fading the ball, drawing the ball, and obviously amusing himself as a great musician exploits his fancies on violin or piano in lighter moments of practice. The little Englishman gave Bobby a pretty lesson on his home course, East Lake; the last time the Southern open was held there until 1927, when Bobby was in the rôle of teacher.

The United States open championship at the fine old Inverness Club of Toledo was held rather later than usual in 1920; August 10-13. Bobby went there in the same light-hearted frame of mind in which he entered less formidable competitions; he had not yet made certain of the vast difference between golf and tournament golf, especially in a national open. And for the qualifying rounds he was paired with Harry Vardon, the Old Master, winner of six British open championships, and the great stylist of his generation. They made a fine pair for the gallery to follow, the oldest and the youngest competitors, and their second round produced one of the funniest and most characteristic anecdotes of golf.

They were tied at the end of the first round, due to Bobby's missing the green of the last hole with a pitch and taking a bad 6 while Vardon stuck his own pitch close for a birdie 3. Bobby was leading the veteran in the second round when they came to the seventh hole, an interesting and even exciting affair, laid out to be played around an angle of tall trees, which the bolder and stronger contestants were carrying with a towering drive from the tee, to place the ball in front of the small green.

Vardon and Bobby each made the big carry successfully and the balls lay some forty yards short of the green, Bobby's slightly ahead. Vardon played a conservative little run-up shot, close to the flag, and Bobby, though there was nothing in the line, elected to pitch delicately with a niblick; a pretty shot, and effective, when it works. In this instance it did not work. Bobby half-topped the ball, which scuttled over the green like a rabbit into much trouble beyond.

He played out with the loss of a stroke to par, and, his ears flaming with embarrassment, walked along beside Vardon toward the next tee. Vardon always was a silent competitor when engaged in serious play. He had not spoken thus far in the round. And Bobby, with an idea of breaking the ice, and at the same time alleviating his own embarrassment, decided to open a conversation.

"Mr. Vardon," he asked bashfully, "did you ever see a worse shot than that?"

"No," said Harry. It was a simple answer, but explicit. And the incident seemed to be closed.

In the championship competition next day, Bobby having qualified easily, he speedily discovered that qualifying rounds were one thing and the championship quite another. He did not know what was the matter—it was a new strain bearing down on him, of course—but the shots wouldn't seem to go right and he wound up with a depressing 78, far down the list, and nine strokes back of Jock Hutchison, popularly known as the Hutch, who led the field with a 69. In the next round he did somewhat better, with a 74, but at the halfway mark he still seemed to be well out of the chase. Hutchison was leading, with 145; Leo Diegel, a young American professional in his first national championship, was second, with 146; and Walter Hagen, open champion of 1919, was tied with Harry Vardon and Ted Ray, at 147.

Seven strokes back of the leader, with his 152, Bobby concluded, boy-like, that he had no chance at all. This relieved his mind of the curious strain of the first two rounds, and when his score went up on the big board at the end of the third round he had done a fine 70.

There is a lot of psychology in golf, and most of all in the grim progress of a major medal-play championship. Bobby looked over the board as his score was posted. Vardon was now leading the field, with 218; Diegel and Hutchison were a stroke behind him, at 219; Ted Ray was next with 220. Bobby, at 222, was tied with Long Jim

Barnes, and was a stroke better than the only other amateur entry of note, Chick Evans.

And he now was only four strokes behind the lead; he had a chance, with one round left to play!

His young blood fired by the prospect, Bobby went to the club's dining-room and fortified himself with a liberal luncheon consisting largely of pie and ice-cream—the worst thing he could have done. And as he ate, he considered the situation. He did not know then, as he learned later, how the terrific pressure of the finishing round of an open championship can break down the game of even the best golfer and most courageous competitor. He could not imagine that in the last round at Inverness every one of the men who were leading him would slip away from Old Man Par to a 75 or worse. He himself had done a 70 in the third round. Now (he told himself) he must go out and do another 70—or better. Very well— and now another segment of pie with ice-cream on it, to strengthen him. Besides, he liked it.

And now the strain was on again; he had a chance. And once more his shots most unaccountably strayed; once more the putts refused to sink. A misguided ambition, and pie *à la mode*, brought in a card of 77. For Bobby's real chance, though he was far from knowing it, lay not in a final round of 70 or better. It lay in stepping along with Old Man Par, while the pressure was breaking the leaders.

A score of 72—level 4's, in the mode of Old Man Par—would have won for Bobby Jones in the last round the first national open championship he entered.

Vardon, fifty years old and tiring fast, had the championship in his pocket, as the saying is, with seven holes left to play. Then a sudden gale sprang up fairly in his face as he confronted the long twelfth hole. It subsided quickly, but it blew Harry Vardon out of his last chance at an American championship. Simple par on three of those last seven holes would have won for him. He got his par on only one—the last. He lost a stroke a hole on the preceding six. His finishing round was a tragic 78. Ted Ray, whose 75 was less of a collapse than the round of other leaders, won with a score of 295. Diegel and the Hutch, each with 77, were tied for second place, a single stroke back of Ray, with Vardon and Jack Burke; four men within a stroke of the winner in the most dramatic finish the American open has yet afforded.

Chick Evans, with a 75, nosed out Bobby for

the position of leading amateur, and Bobby was tied with a professional, Willie Macfarlane, in eighth place with a score of 299. Walter Hagen, 1919 champion, fell back in a bad third round and finished with 301.

"It was as fine a thing as ever happened to me," Bobby told me, years later. "If I had won that first open, I might have got the idea that it was an easy thing to do!"

Be that as it may, pondering that open and some others in the next few years brought Bobby Jones to a very sage conclusion, and one which he found singularly useful in similar affairs.

"Somewhere in an open championship," Bobby reflected, "everybody blows up—if not in the third round, then in the fourth!"

And because Bobby most certainly included himself, when he said everybody, the moral to *that* is, When you find yourself blowing up, just remember that the other fellows are blowing up, too, and keep your own lid on as tight as you can!

CHAPTER X

L ESS than a month after the stirring battle at Inverness, Bobby went to the New York district to play in the national amateur of 1920 at the Engineers Country Club, Roslyn, Long Island. It was his third appearance in that championship, and, I think, the last time he engaged in any major competition with the carefree and light-hearted attitude of his earlier boyhood in golf. After 1920, Bobby took his major golf engagements more and more seriously; each succeeding event became less and less "just another tournament."

Our British cousins like to criticize us good-naturedly on the serious attitude of Americans toward competitive sport; they say we try too hard to win; that we make too much of a business of our preparation; and that our efforts in the competitions are of so severe and even grim a

determination as to rob the sport of all or most of
the enjoyment it is designed to afford. And it is
true that Americans tend to specialize in sport,
rather than to play a number of games accepta-
bly; and I fear it also is true that sometimes
American competitors give the impression of
being too eager to win—after all, no cosmic
catastrophe impends, no national calamity even,
should our crack relay team take second place,
or even third, in an Olympiad; or should some
alien discobolus hurl a spinning platter a whole
yard farther than our best endeavor. But certainly I am not apologizing for any American's
giving his best effort to win in any competitive
sporting event, either against other Americans
or against international adversaries. Rather, I
think, there is a measure of discourtesy to a
worthy foeman in giving anything less than the
best; and most especially, in losing, to suggest
that, after all, it was only a game, and played for
the fun there was in it. Anyway, it is the American idea to play always to win, in any game. And
the only suggestion I should put forward is that,
in formal sporting competition as well as in the
casual encounters that really are mainly for fun,
the true sportsman can never appear offensively
eager in his quest of victory, or to gloat on its

attainment, or to brood too much upon defeat. Which, of course, is nothing, after all, but proper manners.

How much good manners in sport may temper British criticism of American keenness to win is shown by the astonishing popularity of Bobby Jones in the British Isles, where he got away on the wrong foot in one of his first appearances and later went on to win four major championships and help to win for the American side two international matches. Certainly no golfing competitor, American or British or of other nationality, ever tried harder to win championships in Britain, or with more uniform success. Yet Bobby, in learning to try his hardest, after the American fashion, also learned not to seem too eager, too greedy about winning. And on the replica of the great silver cup emblematic of the British amateur championship, presented to him by certain fellow-members of the Royal and Ancient Golf Club of St. Andrews after Bobby announced his retirement from competition, this legend is engraved:

"A Golfer Matchless In Skill, and Chivalrous In Spirit."

Back in 1920, however, Bobby was still looking for fun in national tournaments; he was still learning the lesson that there are two kinds of golf—golf, and tournament golf. He was eighteen years old, still addicted to pie *à la mode* for luncheon between rounds; and otherwise essaying to play golf in a major championship pretty much as he would play it in a pleasant little invitation tournament back home.

The American amateur championship of 1920 offered a marked international aspect. Among the entrants were three Englishmen—Cyril Tolley, amateur champion of Great Britain; Roger Wethered and Lord Charles Hope; and a clever Scottish amateur, Tommy Armour, who proved to be the only one of the quartet to qualify. We shall see more of Mr. Tolley and Mr. Wethered in this narrative; also of Mr. Armour—he became a professional a few years after this tournament and won at various times the open and professional championships of the United States and the open championship of Great Britain; all the major titles to which an American professional (Tommy having become an American) is eligible.

At Roslyn, however, Tommy had a puzzling time qualifying; he got in with a couple of strokes to spare; won his first two matches, and was defeated in the third round by Francis Ouimet, after which the former open and amateur champion encountered Bobby Jones.

Bobby played very well in the two qualifying rounds, one at the North Shore Country Club and the other at the Engineers, and with Freddie Wright of Boston shared the medalist honors with a score of 154, which seems pretty high in these days when that figure will be just about good enough to get you into the charmed circle without a play-off. Still, it was raining and blowing a good deal at both courses, and the top score to get in was 165.

In the first two rounds Bobby met old friends, Simpson Dean, of Rome, Ga., now a Princeton student; and Frank Dyer, whom Bobby had defeated in a great battle in the second round of his first national amateur at Merion. He beat them both handily, by the same score, 5-4, and went into the third round with Freddie Wright. They were about the same age, both rather cocky youngsters, and they were co-medalists—a further inspiration to rivalry. Indeed, they agreed before the match that the winner should have the gold medal emblematic of leading qualifier.

I do not recall any other match in an important competition in which I beheld as many 3's as those two boys showed the gallery in the morning round. Freddie started by sinking a 30-foot putt at the first green for a birdie 3, where Bobby was taking a bad 5. Bobby squared with a birdie 3 at the second. They halved the third in par 4, and Freddie went up again with a birdie 3 at the fourth. Freddie slipped at the fifth and Bobby won it with a par 4, and then touched off three 3's in succession under Freddie, who reached the turn in 35, par for the nine holes, and was 2 down. Bobby did eight 3's in the morning round, and ended the match at the short fourteenth, known at that era as the "2-or-20" hole because of the ease with which one might achieve either figure. Here Bobby stuck a niblick pitch a foot from the flag for a deuce, and ended his third consecutive match in that tournament with the margin of 5-4.

This put him in the semi-final round with Francis Ouimet, and Francis, in the most solemn and kindly manner imaginable, gave Bobby a thoroughly workmanlike spanking. . . . It was at the seventh green of the afternoon round that the boyish spirit of Bobby Jones cropped out for the last time, so far as my observation goes, in an important competition.

Francis had finished the morning round 3 up, Bobby having missed a two-foot putt for a half at the home hole; and Bobby, playing desperately, was unable to close with the tall Bostonian. At the seventh green, Ouimet's ball lay above the flag, some twenty feet away, and Bobby's was somewhat farther away, toward the front of the green and below the cup. As he prepared to putt, rimmed by the largest gallery that had ever followed him, a bee came buzzing along and alighted on the ball. Bobby shooed it away. As he got ready again, back came the bee. He shooed it away again. The persistent insect then settled on the green a couple of yards from the ball and a gallery official popped a megaphone down on top of it. The gallery was beginning to giggle. It roared frankly when the bee at once emerged from the small end of the megaphone and began looking for Bobby once more. Bobby, laughing himself, removed his cap, swung at the bee vigorously, and chased it off the green. Everybody was laughing in the gallery. I think even Francis smiled a bit, but I'm not sure.

Anyway, Bobby, his concentration fairly destroyed, went back to the ball, made a wretched approach putt, missed the next, lost the hole, and was beaten, 6-5, at the thirteenth green of the round, the thirty-first hole of the match. The bee, of course, didn't cost Bobby the battle, by any means. But I've always fancied that insect flew

A VISIT TO BRITAIN

away with a lot of Bobby's juvenile attitude toward what we are pleased to term serious golf.

Chick Evans, champion of 1916, went on to defeat Ouimet next day in the final round before a gallery of 13,000, achieving a brilliant revenge for the tremendous battle in which Francis had beaten him at the last green at Oakmont the year before. Chick was playing in his best form after the first nine holes in which both were uncertain, and after the morning round Francis hadn't a chance.

But the object-lesson at Engineers came in the second round, when Chick appeared hopelessly beaten, and Bobby, his own match finished successfully, saw what he vaguely assumed to be the workings of destiny.

After winning his first-round match easily, defeating F. C. Newton of Boston 8-7, Evans met Reginald Lewis, and Reggie was playing strong and aggressive golf. It was a ding-dong bout all the way, but going to the thirty-sixth tee Evans was 1 down—with one to play. Lewis's drive was straight and Chick pulled to a bunker, and his recovery was a hundred yards short of the green, the ball lying in clover—a difficult shot, in any event. Reggie's second was just over the green, a couple of yards up a slope beyond. Chick played a

133

fine pitch from the clover, and his ball held the green, five yards from the flag—but all Lewis had to do, to win the match, was to get a half. Reggie took some time over his chip-shot and Evans was so nervous he could not stand still. He walked off to one side to be out of Reggie's vision and paced back and forth, back and forth. Lewis chipped not too well, but closer than Evans. Chick now had to sink his putt, and Reggie miss his, to keep the match alive.

Chick sank his putt—a curving rainbow—and tottered off the green and dropped on the turf. Lewis missed. The match was square. They halved the first four extra holes. Evans won at the forty-first. He was that near to defeat in the second round. And he went on to win the championship with never another close match. He beat Fownes 7-6, Allis 10-8, and Ouimet 7-6.

I think it was right there that Bobby began to feel that there really might be a destiny that shapes the ends of golf. The professionals have a way of saying of a winner, "It was *his* tournament."

The amateur championship of 1920 was Chick Evans's tournament, surely.

After that championship Bobby went over to the Morris County Country Club and won an in-

vitation tournament, and then he and Chick
Evans defeated Harry Vardon and Ted Ray 10-9
in a 36-hole match; perhaps the worst licking that
celebrated pair ever received. But Bobby could
not work up any cheering for himself over these
successes. He couldn't forget that big tournament at Engineers, just before the little one he
had captured, or that bigger one at Inverness,
where Ray was first and Vardon was second—
and Bobby was eighth.

Invitation tournaments and exhibition matches
were one thing, he reflected. Major championships
were quite another.

Still, by the next spring he was in a happy and
excited frame of mind, setting sail for Britain
with a jolly party of American amateurs, to play
in the British amateur championship at old Hoylake, and—Bobby, at any rate—in the British
open at St. Andrews. It was the first really or-
ganized invasion of the British championship by
American amateurs, and the informal team match
played before the tournament, and won by the
Americans, was the forerunner of the Walker
Cup international match now played biennially,
in alternate countries.

Up around Liverpool were plenty of new things
to see, and not a few new things to learn about

golf. There was the Royal Liverpool course at Hoylake, which was astonishingly dry for that tournament—Bobby learned that they didn't have a system of water-works about the great British courses (links, they are called, when beside the sea on real "links land"; inland courses are not properly termed links) and that the huge greens were dry and lightning fast or wet and slow, at the pleasure of the elements. He learned that one must have a variety of golf, to cope with British conditions; the sweeping sea-breeze bothered him no end; his beautiful, steep pitch shots bounded from the baked putting surfaces as if from cement; and he had not acquired the deft and useful run-up approach that is an absolute necessity in dry and windy weather. . . . The visitors were so dismayed by the greens that, as a concession, several buckets of water were poured about the pin on one of the dryest surfaces, so a golf ball might be eased up and stopped somewhere near the hole—until the water was absorbed.

Bobby and a pleasant opponent named Manford were the first to start in the first round; pairings and starting-times are drawn impartially from a hat, in Britain; and Bobby remembers less about the match than the way the old cab-horse's hooves clop-clopped along the pavement in the very early morning air, going out to the Hoylake course before almost anybody was stirring.

But he played a fine round, close to par, and won his match easily. Then he was alternately bad and good, and when he was bad he was terrible.

Bobby's next adversary was a Mr. Hamlet, and so far as Bobby could tell he was not a melancholy Dane, but a little florist from some Midland town. Mr. Hamlet probably was an excellent florist, but he was not at all a good golfer—at any rate on this occasion. He worked around the Hoylake course with a card of 87, and it may interest a good many well-informed golfers to learn that Bobby Jones once won a match in a national championship with a score of 86—for that is just what Bobby did, defeating Mr. Hamlet 1 up at the home green.

After this he played a good round against Robert Harris, whom he defeated 6-5, and then he collapsed conclusively before a genial, sandy-haired gentleman named Allan Graham, who was wielding a little brass putter with deadly effect on the glassy greens. Bobby lost, 6-5, and Bill Fownes defeated his fellow-American, Chick Evans, the leading hope of the invaders; and Freddie Wright, Bobby's rival the season before in the United States Championship, was the last American, going out in the sixth round before Bernard Darwin, grandson of Charles Darwin, the naturalist, and the most delightful writer of golf in the world.

So old Hoylake, where Bobby won the last of his three British open championships in 1930, taught him in 1921 that he really knew very little about playing golf in a wind; or getting the ball on to greens baked hard and glassy; or putting on such greens when he did get the ball there. And, all in all, it seems he did pretty well to get as far as his fourth match at Hoylake before elimination.

And then, after watching Willie Hunter win the British amateur championship—mentioned especially because he and Willie had a prime argument to settle St. Louis before the year was out—Bobby journeyed over to the Auld Grey City of St. Andrews, there to play in the British open championship over the Old Course, as they call it, alongside the North Sea (formerly the German Ocean) and under the changing skies and the yet more variable breezes of Fife.

If, as the great and wise M. Maeterlinck has suggested, the present and the future really are co-existent, Bobby Jones should have stepped out reverently upon the silken turf of the most famous golf course in the world. He should have loved it at once—for he was to love it beyond all other courses. And certainly he should never have behaved as he did in the British open of 1921; for there in the future, superimposed upon the smooth pastel of the eighteenth green, is the same Bobby Jones carried high on broad Scottish shoulders above a gallery of cheering, scrambling thousands—winner of the British open championship with the lowest score yet recorded.

Bobby couldn't have enjoyed the faintest prevision of this glowing scene, in 1921. For what he did on the occasion of his first visit to St. Andrews was to hate the course enthusiastically; use up 46 strokes on the first nine holes of his third round; start the inward journey with a ghastly 6 at the tenth—and pick up his ball, withdrawing from the competition, just before taking another 6 at the short eleventh.

This is the only instance in Bobby's entire career of giving up play in a formal competition before he was eliminated or the competition was ended. Of course there is no stigma attaching to the withdrawal of a competitor in a medal-play golfing event, when he is not matched with any individual adversary but is playing against the field. Every major open championship has withdrawals, of contestants off their game and scoring hopelessly. And in withdrawing Bobby of course did not cease to play along with the man with whom he was paired for the last two rounds, and keep his companion's score; he simply announced, by the act of picking up his ball at the eleventh green of the third round, that from then on his own score did not count.

And that is the only major competition, or golfing event of any importance, in all his career of which the record is not complete. And I think it also is the only real regret of Bobby Jones's golfing life, that he didn't play out the string, in that first venture at old St. Andrews.

Bobby didn't start too badly, the first day, and at the halfway mark, after rounds of 74 and 78, he was five strokes back of Jock Hutchison, the brilliant Scottish-American professional—he was born at St. Andrews—and at that stage was a stroke ahead of Roger Wethered, the tall English amateur, who, with two great rounds next day, was to end in a tie with Hutchison for first place.

But it was Jock, the transplanted Scot, who startled the world in that first round with an ace —a hole in one shot—at the 142-yard eighth hole, and then smacked a huge drive, with a beautiful "draw" down a quartering wind, clear on to the ninth green; a wallop of 303 yards, the ball touching the rim of the cup and stopping three inches away for an eagle—so near it was to being two aces in succession! Jock cut away four strokes from Old Man Par in those two holes; and while he slipped away from his 70 in the morning to a 77 in the afternoon, he retained the lead until Wethered next morning went away with a round that was better than par while the Hutch slipped farther back, with a 79.

So it came about that Wethered, finishing early in the afternoon with another grand round, left the Hutch, as he started out on his own last lap, the terrific problem of doing a flat 70 on a par-73 course—and that course St. Andrews— to tie. And that problem, whether you know it or not, is the very toughest in all golf; to know what you have to do, a whole round in advance. Especially when the mark is better than par.

Hutchison did it. He shot the 70. That round forever will be ranked with the favored candidates when the traditional debate begins as to which was the greatest round of golf ever played.

Bobby watched much of that round. And he had played with the Hutch when Jock did the eighth and ninth holes 1-2. And he was playing directly back of Roger Wethered when Roger committed the little fault that cost him the championship—backing down from a mound he had climbed to get his line to the sixteenth green, he stepped on his ball in the long grass. The penalty, one stroke, left him in a tie with Hutchison, who beat him next day in the play-off.

"My feet are just too big," was Roger's comment, with a smile. Not a word of complaint; not a hint of bad luck. Sportsmen, these English!

So Bobby, while he was learning from his own petulance that it is best to play out even a sorry string, learned something from the Hutch, and something from Roger, and something from old St. Andrews. A lot, from old St. Andrews. He did not, it must be confessed, learn to love St. Andrews then. But he learned to respect it. And that, we are told, is the best foundation for true love.

CHAPTER XI

THE British excursion, in 1921, completed one phase of Bobby Jones's experience in the Big Show. He had now played in all of the four championships which compose it. At the age of nineteen years and four months he had competed in three United States amateur championships, one United States open, one British amateur, and one British open. And the golfing year of 1921, like the calendar year, was only half over. Before Bobby was more than half through telling the home folks about his visit to Britain he was starting out again on the long trail, this time to the Columbia Country Club at Washington, where the national open championship was played July 19-22.

This tournament was remarkable for two things. Long Jim Barnes won it with the widest margin of modern times—nine strokes ahead of

Walter Hagen and Freddie McLeod, who were tied for second place, and for the first and last time a qualifying test of a single 18-hole round was played to establish the field to compete in the championship proper. Until this tournament, and thereafter, until the present system of regional qualification was adopted, the contestants met at the field of, battle and played a medal test of 36 holes to qualify a certain number, usually 60 and ties for the sixtieth place, for the championship. When the entry list grew too large for all to play on a single day, the field was divided into sections, and each section played 36 holes on a separate day.

At Washington there were 262 entries and 258 starters; and for some reason, never at all clear to me, it was decided to play the qualifying test in two sections, and at a single round of 18 holes.

Certainly this plan was not suggested by any such demand by the contestants, who, to a man, deplored it bitterly. You see, in a single round where a crack field is competing for places in the championship, a single bad hole—a single bit of ill fortune, is likely to keep a worthy competitor out of the tournament. At 36 holes, luck has a chance to readjust its breaks, and the really expert players are to a great extent masters of their destiny.

Everybody was nervous, starting that qualifying round, and I suppose nobody was any more nervous than Bobby Jones and Leo Diegel, the young professional who was so near to winning the open championship of 1920, finishing in a tie for second place at his first start. He and Bobby had grown to be great friends; they had entered this branch of the Big Show the same season; they played together at Columbia in practice; and they were paired for the qualifying round in their own section of the field.

I suppose Leo was the more nervous of the two; probably the most nervous player in the entire field. But it was Bobby who almost wrecked his chances of qualification at the very first shot and thus spoiled a record I mentioned with some complacency in an earlier chapter—the record of never having failed to qualify for any major championship in which he was entered.

The first hole at the Columbia Country Club is a dog-leg, bending to the right. Bobby got hold of his drive with a terrific hook that sent the ball curving far to the left, deep into a forest of the type usually described in the story books as impenetrable.

I was conscious of a vast sinking sensation back of my belt buckle as the gallery went pelting down from the high tee and along the narrow fairway. Bobby was in bad, right at the jump. If he could not find the ball he would have to go back to the tee and drive over, with a penalty of stroke and distance—that is, he would be playing his third shot. If he did find the ball it might be unplayable—also a two-stroke penalty. If it was playable, he might hit a tree with his next shot, and—well, I was worried until I could feel my hair turning gray. It is such a terrible thing, not to qualify. Not winning a tournament—you get used to that. And only one player can win. But not to *qualify*—I tried to dismiss the prospect, and hobbled into the forest, which was not quite impenetrable.

The ball was found, all right. And there was an opening in the trees toward the green, which might be reached by a firm iron shot right over a huge prostrate tree trunk some ten yards in front of the ball.

Bobby, relieved by finding the situation not so bad as he had feared, concluded to go for the green and possibly get away without losing even one stroke. No ambition ever met a prompter rebuke. I think, too, he was subjectively aware

146

of his folly as he made the shot, employing an iron instead of a well-lofted pitching club. He flinched ever so slightly as he came on the ball.

Cr-r-rack! It struck the prostrate giant of the forest fairly in the ribs. And as other sounds of impact between hard rubber and forestry indicated the swift if eccentric movement of the ball to somewhere else behind us, I heard the man next to me in the gallery say, under his breath:

"There goes Bobby!"

And it was like an echo of the words that were forming in my own mind. It seemed indeed that Bobby was gone, so far as a chance for qualification was concerned.

But the ball was found again, this time without any open path toward the green, or, indeed, the fairway. Cooled and steadied by the increasing strain, Bobby figured out the thinnest patch of foliage, chose a mashie-niblick, and played the only shot that might help him—a tremendous pitch, hit with all his power, in the hope that the ball might rip through to safety.

It did. It barely reached the fairway, but it was out of the woods. And Bobby played out the hole for a 6, and was duly thankful to get it, though two strokes were gone to par, right at the start.

He knew now that he could not afford to waste anything more, and he stuck to his work with desperate concentration. One other emergency arose. At the seventeenth hole, a drive and a steep pitch to a hilltop green, the pitch failed to get up and the ball came rolling back down the bluff. Bobby pitched again, not too well—and he had to sink a 30-foot putt for his par 4.

This was the only time Bobby Jones ever was close to a failure in the qualifying round of any important competition. He got into the national open of 1921, but he had not a single stroke to spare.

Bobby's play in the ensuing championship was the most erratic of his career. His first round was an extraordinarily wild 78, nine strokes back of Jim Barnes, who, with a 69, had set out to spread-eagle the field. In the second round Bobby got going. He played the first nine holes for an incredibly brilliant 32 and it looked as if anything might happen—he might even take the lead away from Barnes, for at one time he seemed to have a fine chance to do a 65, and Barnes was slipping far away from his own first round. Then, with half a dozen holes to play, Bobby fairly exploded. He lost what is termed a hatful of strokes—six at the least—and still finished with a 71, gaining four strokes on Barnes, who did a 75.

This left Bobby five strokes from the lead, and next morning in his third round he played up to the greens in beautiful fashion and there he missed putts of every conceivable range. In one of the strangest and most exasperating rounds of his career he used 37 strokes in reaching the greens and 40 putts thereafter; he was putting for a birdie on every green except two—and he finished with a ghastly 77.

Starting the final round, Bobby again was nine strokes back of Barnes and of course there was nothing to do but shoot the works. Par on the first five holes at Columbia was 4-4-4-3-5. Bobby started 3-3-4-3-9.

Clipping two strokes from par on the first four holes, Bobby got a great drive on the 560-yard fifth, a par 5; went for the green with a big brassie, pulled out of bounds; tried again, pulled out of bounds; played the next one carefully down the right-hand side of the fairway, took a 9 on the hole, and was through. He played out patiently for another 77 and a total of 303, a tie in fifth place with Alex Smith—the oldest and the youngest competitor—and a stroke behind his now inveterate rival among the amateurs, Chick Evans, who never again finished ahead of him in an open championship.

Long Jim Barnes finished in easy fashion with a score of 289, doing his last round in 72. President Harding and Vice-President Coolidge were seated at the home green, where Mr. Harding, an ardent golfer, himself presented the gold medal and the big cup. . . . I stood within three yards of the President while Joe Kirkwood was giving an exhibition of trick shots, waiting for Barnes to finish, and after a mild altercation with a Secret Service man I made a very good picture of Mr. Harding with a small camera I always carried.

I rode back to the hotel with Walter Hagen, who had tied with Freddie McLeod for second place.

"Bobby was playing some great golf, in spots," said Walter. "He's got everything he needs to win any championship except experience, and maybe philosophy. He's still a bit impetuous. But I'll tip you off to something—Bobby will win the open before he wins the amateur!"

And this was a prophecy.

Two months later Bobby and I were on a train going out to St. Louis, where the national amateur championship was to be played, Sep-

tember 17-24. In those days we didn't have draw-
ing-rooms and compartments. We had lower
berths when we could get them and uppers when
we couldn't, and no grousing about it. While my
berth was being made down in a crowded car I
sat with Bobby in his berth and we talked about
the amateur championship.

Bobby said, "I wonder if I'm *ever* going to win
one of these things."

I said, "Bobby, if you ever get it through your
head that whenever you step out on the first tee
of any competition you are the best golfer in it,
then you'll win this championship and a lot of
others."

It sounds a rather terrible thing to tell a youngster not yet twenty, of course. But Bobby, essentially a modest boy, was by way of getting what
they call an inferiority complex, through a steady
series of beatings. And it was my honest conviction then, as it has remained since, that Bobby
was the best golfer in the world.

He laughed, rather ruefully, and begged me
not to be an idiot.

"I've seen these chaps play," he said. "They're
good. They're awfully good. And I know it."

I had one more try.

"Bobby," I said, "I've seen them play, too. All

of them. And I've seen you play, which you never have done. And I tell you you're better. And the sooner you believe it the sooner you'll win."

But Bobby only laughed again. He didn't believe it then. If he ever came to believe it, he never admitted the conviction. As I said, he was always a modest boy. He still is a modest boy. But whether Bobby ever came to regard himself as the best golfer in the world—if there can be such a ranking—a great many other people were convinced of it, before he hung up his clubs, after the season of 1930.

On the way to St. Louis, Bobby also had the western open championship to ponder, along with the national open, and the British experiences. Bobby had played in the western open with a lot of the leading professionals, at the Oakwood Club near Cleveland. He had started with a rush of beautiful golf and was leading the field at the end of the first day's play, of 36 holes. Then came a fine, stiff breeze—the kind you get in Britain. And Bobby's experience overseas had not as yet been assimilated; he blew up spectacularly in the third round while Walter Hagen, one of the game's greatest masters of adverse conditions, went on to win with a score of 287. With 294,

Bobby was tied with Joe Kirkwood in fourth place.

At the St. Louis Country Club, Bobby once more appeared headed for a championship—even more so than at Oakmont, where he had reached the finals in 1919. He qualified easily with a score of 151, seven strokes behind the medalist, Francis Ouimet, and a round dozen strokes under the top score. He beat his first opponent, Clarence Wolff, 12-11, and his second, Dr. O. F. Willing, 9-8, and in the third round his opponent was none other than Willie Hunter—the same little Englishman who had won the British amateur championship at Hoylake, where Bobby was a victim of a bewilderingly dry course, British breezes, and the little brass putter of Mr. Allan Graham.

Willie had had a terrific battle with James Manion in the previous round; the St. Louis course was damp and slow and he was not getting much run on his rather abbreviated tee shots, and the general opinion was that Bobby would take the British champion in his stride and meet either Bob Gardner or Rudy Knepper in the next round.

I think Bobby was of this opinion himself. He afterward confessed that he was somewhat surprised when they went in to luncheon after the

first round and he was only 2 up. He was out-
ranging Hunter greatly from the tee and the rest
of his game was working well enough, save for a
tendency of his ball, landing on the green from
steep pitches with backspin, to pick up mud from
the damp surface and make the putting uncertain
for him. Yet he was only 2 up, and the British
champion was sticking to him like a bulldog.

Bobby didn't know it at the time, but while he
was out-driving Hunter, the little Englishman
was out-thinking him. He noticed after a while
that Hunter's ball never had any mud on it when
he came to putt; and it was Willie's superb putting that was keeping him in the battle. But Bobby
failed to connect the clean ball on the green with
the low, running shots employed by Hunter to get
it there, in place of the more spectacular American style of pitching with backspin, to stop the
ball almost in its tracks. And even if Bobby had
noticed the difference, he had not yet acquired
command of the running approach without which
a golfer is singularly helpless on most British
courses. Curiously enough, this type of approach
is equally useful on a very dry, fast course or
on a soggy course—unless the tournament committee gives permission to clean the ball after

reaching the putting surface, as sometimes is done.

So Hunter was using his head and a running approach, and Bobby was using a fine pitch with backspin, and the match continued to be a great dog-fight in the afternoon. Bobby was still 2 up as he stood on the eighth tee; 2 up, with eleven holes to play, and the Englishman hanging to him with true English tenacity. And there Bobby had an idea.

The eighth hole at the St. Louis Country Club is played from a very high tee on a hillcrest to a small green hidden away behind tall trees in a sharp angle to the right. It measures 347 yards, a drive-and-pitch, the way it is laid out. In practice, Bobby had been experimenting with a long, towering drive straight over the trees toward the green, and several times he had reached the putting surface and achieved an easy birdie 3. It was an extremely perilous manœuvre, as a deep, wide ditch guarded the green on that side and the drive had to go all the way in the air.

Bobby knew that Hunter hadn't the range for such a shot, and, insensibly irked by the Englishman's persistence, he suddenly made up his mind to try the big jump again. He felt sure he could bring off the shot, and, if he did, an almost cer-

tain 3 might very well break Willie's stubborn
back.

In the same situation in later years Bobby
would calmly have continued his own private battle with Old Man Par, letting the human opponent, who was behind, take the chances. But this
was St. Louis, in 1921. And Bobby, facing around
on the hillcrest tee, discharged a huge, towering
drive straight over the top of the tallest tree in
the angle.

It was a twig no larger than a pencil that broke
up that golf match and, many critics fancy,
stopped Bobby Jones's march to a major championship. Caught at the peak of its flight by the
topmost branch of the tallest tree, the ball came
down like a wounded bird in the ditch full of
stones and undergrowth. The first blast produced
a desperately scared rabbit, but no ball. . . . Hunter won that hole, and the next one. Bobby's play
never resumed its smooth mechanical precision.
He went up again at the long thirteenth; Hunter
squared with a 30-foot putt for a birdie 3 at the
fourteenth, and himself went up at the fifteenth,
where Bobby missed a putt of less than a yard.
Each had a putt of ten feet at the Redan—and
Hunter sank his to become dormie 2. Bobby
missed a five-yard putt for a birdie 3 at the next

hole, the thirty-fifth of the match, and they shook hands.

"I can play this game only one way," Bobby told me, late that night at the hotel. "I must play every shot for all there is in it."

But, also in his own way, Bobby worked around slowly and surely to another theory of the game. At St. Louis, as on many another field, his bold, dashing play endeared him to galleries and critics alike; he was the D'Artagnan of golf—the fiery young cavalier ignoring his guard to drive home the finishing thrust. He was beating many a worthy foeman brilliantly. But he was not winning any championships.

And before he started on the string that in the seven fat years tied together forty victories in major tournament matches, with only three defeats, the young D'Artagnan had to learn and take deeply to heart the wisdom of an older cavalier, who once said to him:

"The best shot, Bobby, is not always the one to play."

He had to learn, too, that matching shots with the most debonair of human adversaries is at the best a feeble and uncertain pattern, compared with the iron certitudes of Old Man Par.

CHAPTER XII

OF ALL the returnings home after golfing pilgrimages, I have little doubt that the dreariest one for Bobby Jones was the long journey back to Atlanta from Boston, in September, 1922. Oddly enough, it was the last homeward journey from defeat in the last of the seven lean years, in which Bobby had played in ten major championships without a victory. The next time he started back to Atlanta from a tournament in the Big Show he would be carrying a large gold medal and an old silver cup, emblematic of the open championship of the United States. But of course Bobby didn't know this when he boarded the train at Boston. What he did know was that, in his fifth start in the national amateur championship, Jess Sweetser had given him the most decisive beating of his career, in the semi-final round at Brookline. It seemed to be no use at all.

HIS FIRST NATIONAL AMATEUR CHAMPIONSHIP
—MERION, 1916

HIS FIRST VISIT TO ENGLAND FOR BRITISH
AMATEUR AND BRITISH OPEN—1921

Nothing seemed any use. Big Bob and I agreed thoroughly on this, before we started home. Bobby himself had little to say. The gloom in that section of the Pullman was sufficiently dense to make conversation more of an effort than it appeared to be worth.

And yet the season of 1922, the last of the lean years, started hopefully enough, though the curtain rose on a scene in an Atlanta hospital, where Bobby, tired of the painful annoyance of sundry patches of swollen veins in his left leg, went for an operation less than a month before the tournament program opened for him with the southern amateur championship, once more played at his home club, East Lake.

Bobby was an extremely busy young man at this juncture. He was being graduated from the Georgia School of Technology and planning to enter Harvard in quest of a B.S. degree after the tournament season, and prior to *that* came the operation, or, rather, four operations simultaneously, on his ailing left leg.

In all probability Bobby would not have entered the southern, even at his home club, had it not been for the George W. Adair Memorial Trophy, put in play for the first time at that championship; a tall, beautiful, eminently dignified emblem given by the golfers of Atlanta as a perpetual award of the southern association in memory of Perry Adair's father, who had died two years earlier—a great sportsman who had done incalculable service for golf in Atlanta and in the south, and, as you may remember, had encouraged Bobby's career from its beginning. Bobby had a feeling that this might be the last southern amateur championship in which he would compete—as, indeed, it was—and he wanted very much to have his name on the great trophy dedicated to the memory of his dear friend. He was out of the hospital less than a fortnight before the tournament started; the doctor forbade him to play a complete round in practice, and his preparation for the last start in the southern amateur consisted of four hours, spread over suitable intervals, on the practice tee, and one excursion of nine holes— halfway around the East Lake course.

If this unusual preliminary training was responsible for what happened in the tournament, I can think of a number of other events where an operation and a hospital sojourn would have been helpful.

The East Lake course at that time was 6,700 yards around, with a par of 72. Bobby qualified with a card of 75 in a triple tie with Perry Adair and "Tub" Palmer, of Miami, and went on to win the championship without being really threatened in a single match. At the conclusion of the tournament, his total score, including the 75 of the medal round, was ten strokes better than par. Bobby's name was the first to go on the memorial trophy; Perry won it the next year, at Birmingham; and thus their names are together—the two boys in whose golf George Adair found his greatest interest. Bobby never played in the championship again.

Some weeks later, his leg fully recovered, Bobby set out for the Skokie Country Club, at Glencoe, Ill., not far from Chicago, to play in the national open championship. He was accompanied by Stewart Maiden, now back at his old post with the East Lake club after a sojourn in St. Louis, and they found a bone-dry, hard-baked course on which the prospective combatants were hitting prodigious drives and turning in some curious scores—in practice. Par at Skokie was an unsymmetrical 34-36—70, the field of 320 starters qualified in three sections on separate days—and they played 36 holes in qualifying, this time—and before the tournament got going a terrific rain soaked the course and altered conditions to such an extent that the preliminary rehearsals were of

next to no value. Bobby's best cards in practice
were a couple of rounds in 74; his qualifying
rounds were 72 and 76; and Jock Hutchison led
the field in the preliminary test with startling per-
formances of 67 and 68, setting a record for
qualification scores in the national open, and, apparently having got it all out of his system, turned
in cards of 78 and 74 as his first rounds of the
championship proper.

Walter Hagen, just back from winning the
British open championship, and playing with
Bobby the first two rounds, promptly went to
the front with a card of 68. Bobby, with a modest
74, was six strokes behind him at the luncheon
intermission—and collared Sir Walter at the
tenth green of the afternoon round. Hagen was
in five bunkers on the first nine holes, while
Bobby, whose irons were uncertain all through
the tournament, saved himself by some beautiful
putting.

At the halfway mark, however, it was old John
Black, a California Scot, a grandfather, and one
of the finest shot-makers that ever came out of
Caledonia, who was leading the pack with beau-
tifully symmetrical rounds of 71-71—142. Wild
Bill Mehlhorn was second, with 73-71—144; Ha-

gen and Gene Sarazen were next, tied at 145; and Bobby was fifth, with 74-72—146.

Now, this was not at all an unfavorable position for the Georgia amateur. He was four strokes back of the lead, with two rounds to play; and his game appeared to be improving. The only reason for anxiety I could see was in the fact that a normal putting stride, 32 putts in the morning round, had netted him only a 74; and his improved 72 of the afternoon was extracted from a really erratic assortment of wood and iron play by some superb putting; he used only 28 strokes on the greens.

Still, he was up with the leaders. And next morning, paired with George Duncan, the famous Black Scot, Bobby broke away in brilliant fashion. The putts were dropping again and the other shots were working better, and when he went in to luncheon he left a par 70 on the board—and he was tied with Wild Bill Mehlhorn for first place, at 216. John Black had slipped back to a 75; his three-round total was 217. Hagen's 74 placed him next, with 219; and little Gene Sarazen, with a 75, seemed pretty well out of it at 220, four strokes back of the leaders, and starting out on his last round with a mere handful of gallery as Bobby came in from his third round.

Bobby was in an excellent frame of mind. He felt—though of course he did not say so—that he had come on his game at the best possible time. He had produced rounds of 74, 72 and 70, in that order; he was tied for the lead, and (he confessed this later) he had it firmly in mind that he could do a 68 for the last round, thus concluding a symmetrical improvement. And that, he was warrantably certain, would be good enough to win.

A 68 would have been amply good enough to win, for Bobby, tied for the lead as the last round began. As it turned out, a 68 was good enough to win for Gene Sarazen—starting that round four strokes behind. It was Gene who did the 68. And he finished early; his score went on the board just as Bobby went to the tenth tee, having used 36 strokes on the first nine holes. Bobby's chance for a 68 had passed, for the last nine was the harder side, at Skokie. And before he had played the tenth hole he knew what he had to do—a par 36 to tie Sarazen; a 35 on the last nine to go ahead of him.

If the harsh news shook Bobby's nerves, it did not show in his drive—a huge wallop, well ahead of George Duncan. His iron second rolled just over the green, however, and he chipped back too firmly, ten feet past the hole.

I was standing beside Stewart Maiden as Bobby went for the putt which he needed so desperately for a par 4. He struck it firmly; too firmly. The ball held the line to the cup, touched the rim— switched, and stayed up.

Stewart and I looked at each other under the long, moaning sigh the gallery exudes on such an occasion. The little Scot was ghastly under the tan; his face was set like a flint. He shook his head ever so slightly. Bad business. A stroke was gone where he needed to pick one up, somewhere in that run.

Bobby was working as hard as he ever worked in his life, trying to pick up that stroke, and instead he lost another, pitching over the green at the twelfth, blasting out 30 feet from the flag, and missing the long putt for his par. He had to sink an ugly little four-footer for his par 3 at the thirteenth, after missing the green from the tee. And then, while I was trudging along in the gallery down the fourteenth fairway, after a tremendous drive of Bobby's that nearly reached the green, somebody came up behind me and clapped me on the back.

"Don't let your chin drag," Bobby said. "It's not so bad as all that!"

And I realized suddenly that I must have been

looking pretty glum; but I had no idea he was noticing. I grinned back at him, and he grinned a bit, too. But his face was gray and sunken and his eyes looked an inch deep in his head.

He made a wretched chip—and then sank a 30-foot putt for a birdie 3. And one of the strokes had come back.

He was playing grand golf now, but a putt of five yards just failed to drop for another birdie at the fifteenth; one more turn and the ball would have been in. And the same thing happened after two fine shots at the sixteenth. He stood on the seventeenth tee needing 4-4 to tie Sarazen, and par on those holes was 4-5.

He had been getting a 4 regularly at the long eighteenth, which he could reach with a drive and a spoon. It was the seventeenth that betrayed him—a slightly elbowed two-shotter on which a bold, big drive straight over a towering mound and bunker along the boundary line should be rewarded by a simple and easy iron second to the green, where a safe, conservative drive to the right of the big bunker left a much harder approach.

As always, Bobby went for the bold shot and brought it off perfectly, so far as we could see from the tee. The ball carried well over the bunker and the mound and disappeared as if on a ruled line toward the flag. . . . What caused that ball to bound far out of line to the left I never have learned. But there it was, in a dim sort of roadway, under a tree.

That was the break. Bobby hacked the ball from a nearly impossible position to the front of the sloping green, 160 yards away. His chip up the slope was short. The putt also was short. His 5 at that hole left him an eagle 3 to tie Sarazen at the long finishing hole. He went for it desperately, and his spoon second sent the ball into the gallery at the left of the green. . . . Now he had a wee pitch-and-run for a tie. . . . The ball actually rolled over the cup. It was that close. He sank a six-foot putt for a birdie 4. He was second, a stroke back of Sarazen.

Old John Black, apparently headed for glory with a 33 on the first nine, ran into trouble in several places on the homeward journey, and that same miserable seventeenth tripped him for a 6, which ruined him as it had ruined Bobby, and left them in a tie at 289; the same score which the year before had won for Long Jim Barnes at Columbia, with nine big strokes to spare. This time it was good only for second place. Gene Sarazen was champion.

It was in this championship that Bobby forged definitely to the front among the amateur contestants in open competitions. Chick Evans had nosed him out by a stroke at Inverness and again at Columbia. This time Chick, with a score of 302, was thirteen strokes behind Bobby. Jesse Guilford, who had won the amateur championship at St. Louis the year before, was sixteen strokes behind; and Willie Hunter, who had beaten Bobby at St. Louis, was seventeen strokes back. No amateur ever finished ahead of Bobby again in any open competition.

On the train going home to Atlanta I asked Bobby, consolingly, as I considered, what he'd do if he played as poor a game as I did.

"I'd have a lot more fun out of it," he replied.

Which gave me something to think about.

He was plugging away at Cicero's Orations Against Cataline as we journeyed north and east in August, headed for Southampton, Long Island, where Bobby was to play with the American team in the first of the Walker Cup international matches with Great Britain at the beautiful National Links.

"This bird Cicero," he said once, "was a long way from hating himself. I wish I could think as much of my golf as he did of his statesmanship."

Between his bouts with Cicero we talked about other things—not much about golf. Dr. Einstein had lately propounded some interesting theories, and a little book by an ex-newspaperman, Edwin F. Slosson, had helped me to what I fondly hoped was a sort of idea of the Fourth Dimension. Bobby always was keen about odd scientific facts and fancies, and it was after a grapple with Dr. Einstein's Fourth Dimension (as simplified by Mr. Slosson) that he said a very remarkable thing for a twenty-year-old sport celebrity.

"The thing that bothers me most about this life," said Bobby, "is that there's so little time to learn all the things a fellow wants to know."

At the National Links, however, he laid aside Cicero and Einstein to do battle for flag and country in the Walker match, defeating Roger Wethered, the very tall English amateur, 3-2 in the singles, and, with Jess Sweetser as partner, winning in the foursomes by the same margin from C. V. L. Hooman and W. B. Torrance. The American side won the team match, 8 points to 4. To this date the huge cup has been played for six times, and it has yet to pass out of our possession—which seems a bit piggish, even to an American.

Of the eight American amateurs on the team

of 1922, Jess Sweetser was ranked No. 8. Jesse Guilford, amateur champion, was No. 1, Bobby was No. 2, and Chick Evans was No. 3. All these won their matches at singles against the British, while Sweetser lost his to "Chubby" Hooman. And yet, in the national amateur championship at Brookline, three days later, the twenty-year-old Sweetser walloped his No. 1, No. 2, and No. 3 team-mates in the order named, and the afternoon of September 9, finishing with Chick Evans at the thirty-fourth green, became the amateur champion of the United States.

Evidences of this devastating humor did not appear in the qualifying rounds, which, on the second day, presented absorbing problems of their own. The first round was played under perfect weather conditions; the second for the most part in the hardest rain I ever saw on a golf event. Sweetser qualified neatly enough with a score of 152 for the 36 holes, ten strokes under the top mark and eight strokes behind Guilford, who nosed Jones out for the medal with 74-70—144 to Bobby's 73-72—145, each playing his better round on the rainy day.

Bobby had a hard fight in each of his first three matches. He defeated James J. Beadle 3-1, Bob

Gardner—it was their third meeting—3-2 in the rain; and William McPhail 4-3. Meanwhile, Sweetser had got started in the same bracket on what some of the golf-writers termed a rampage. The course suited his game exactly—half the holes were of the drive-and-pitch variety, and in this tournament Sweetser's pitching clubs were so amazingly accurate that he was hitting the flag-staff frequently from ranges of from 90 to 140 yards. He defeated H. E. Kenworthy 10-9, Willie Hunter 7-6, and Jesse Guilford, 1921 champion and medalist, 4-3.

This brought Yale and Harvard together in the fourth round, and from the second hole it was all Yale.

After a rather sloppy half in 5 at the first green, Bobby hit a slightly longer and straighter drive from the second tee, and Sweetser played the odd. The hole was of 305 yards, up a considerable slope to a small green. Sweetser's drive was pushed out to the right, and left him an uphill pitch of some 90 yards, his target being the upper half of the flag-staff. He walked a few yards up the hill, getting the lay of the land. Then he returned to his ball, set himself, and swung that deadly spade-mashie.

A great part of the big gallery had gone ahead and was massed about the rear of the green. The ball descended sharply, in line with the flag. There was a long moment of dead silence, then a roar like the crash of artillery.

Sweetser had holed out, for an eagle 2.

Bobby grinned, shook his head, played his own pitch.

Another roar—but not a crash. A tribute to a gallant effort. The ball had stopped less than a foot from the flag. But a birdie 3 was no good there.

Sweetser finished that round like a man inspired. He was out in 34 and was 6 up. Bobby played the first nine in a wretched 40. Then he braced for a desperate spurt that carried him the last nine holes in 34, two strokes better than par— and gained back only one hole. He was 5 down at the intermission. Sweetser had set a new course record of 69. He was precisely par on every hole of the afternoon round until the match ended, 8-7, at the eleventh green—a mile from the clubhouse.

In the lower bracket Chick Evans went along smoothly to the finals, and there, in a hard match, Sweetser beat him 3-2.

One week later Bobby Jones set a record that

stands today for the Old Course at his home club, East Lake. He did a 63 against a par of 72. Nine pars. Nine birdies. He was not at all elated.

"The place for that round," he said, "was at Brookline—or Skokie."

CHAPTER XIII

COMING as it did on the heels of the drubbing at Brookline, Bobby did not appear to think much of his record at East Lake the afternoon of Saturday 16, 1922; but it remained to the end of his career the lowest score he ever turned in on a regular course, and to this date it never has been equaled at Bobby's home club. So I am just going to set it down here, against par, so you may see what the figures look like on a big course of 6,700 yards, when a great golfer really gets hot, as the saying is:

```
Par (out) ...... 434  553  435—36
Bobby .......... 324  443  434—31

Par (in) ....... 434  455  443—36—72
Bobby .......... 433  454  333—32—63
```

This was the lowest score Bobby ever made on a full-sized golf course, but it was not the best

BOBBY JONES WITH NATIONAL OPEN CHAM-
PIONSHIP CUP

(*Acme Photo*)

A STUDY IN CONCENTRATION—1923

round he ever played. That came four years later, at the Sunningdale Golf Club, in England. It was a 66 with only one little mistake in it, which cost nothing in the way of strokes. Still, it kept the round from being absolutely perfect in execution. I suppose there never has been a complete round without a mistake, though many will not show a single hole above par.

Soon after the record performance at East Lake, Bobby went to Harvard and was very busy there and happy, and played next to no golf until the early summer of the next year, 1923, when he came home and began trying to get his game in shape for the national open championship at the Inwood Country Club, on Long Island.

This was difficult—indeed, as it appeared, impossible. He had no minor tournament for tuning up, as the southern amateur the year before; and as the date for the open approached and he was unable to get going, Stewart Maiden decided to accompany him to Inwood. And there in practice his game seemed to get worse. Inwood was a long, narrow course, rather ferocious in its punishment of wild play. An odd feature of the first nine was a series of three holes in succession, the shortest of which was 520 yards—each a par 5—followed by two short holes, of par 3. I have always re-

garded Inwood as one of the very toughest
courses on which the national open has been
played, and Bobby in his preliminary play found
it hard to get around under 80. He was more depressed and worried, I think, than ever before—
or since. It seemed, in a way, as if a great load
of responsibility had settled on him. He had been
in major competition now for seven years; this
tournament at Inwood would be his eleventh start
in the Big Show. And all the time, and in every
field, he was rated, first a possibility, then good
enough to win, then a favorite.

And he never had won.

At St. Louis, and more at Brookline, the critics
shook their heads. A great golfer, they said. As
great a shot-maker as ever lived. But—they shook
their heads. What they meant, of course, was that
a champion must have something more than a fine
array of shots. A champion also must have the
ability to make the shots stick together when the
strain, and the need, are greatest.

Bobby looked suddenly older than his twenty-
one years, plugging around the great Inwood
course, working patiently yet with a sort of des-
peration to get the shots going right.

There was little improvement, until the qualifying rounds. Then Bobby responded to the pressure

with a couple of reasonably good scores and assumed his place, paired with Walter Hagen, among the 77 contestants who had earned their position in a field that numbered 355 starters. The schedule called for two rounds Friday and two rounds Saturday.

The Inwood course was tough. In all that field there were only two scores as good as par in the first round—and those were better. Bobby Jones, who usually played well with Hagen, was a stroke above par on the curious first nine, and then, settling down and using only fourteen putts on the next nine, he clicked off the rest of the journey in 33 strokes, for a card of 71. But it was Jock Hutchison who led the chase, with a level 70. And nobody else was as good as par.

In the afternoon, in spite of a very sour 6 at the 530-yard fourth hole—where he took three putts from a dozen feet—Bobby again was out in 38, and, with a par 35 coming home, he posted a 73. With his morning round that gave him 144 at the halfway mark, exactly par. And again little Jock Hutchison beat him a single stroke on the round; The Hutch, with a par 72, finished the day with 142. And in the press tent that evening the golf-writers were predicting that Jock would never be collared. It was his tournament, they said. Bobby

Cruickshank, the tiny, stocky Scottish university man who had come to this country as a lawyer and had taken up the profession of golf instead, was third, with scores of 73-72—145; and only three other contestants were better than 150. Inwood was separating the tigers from the rabbits, as they say in England, without delay.

And now the hard-earned experience of Inverness and Columbia and Skokie began to tell. Bobby's "bad patch" came with the start of the third round, Saturday morning. A string of ghastly 5's, including two penalty strokes, cost him a 41 on the first nine, four strokes above par. Three years before—two years before, Bobby would have concluded it was all over. Now he had learned something. The experience of Inverness was talking to him, as he set down the 5 at the par-3 seventh. They all blow up somewhere, experience was saying. If not in the third round, then in the fourth. They all blow up somewhere, in an open championship. And the thing to do, when you start blowing up, is just to keep the lid on the best you can—the best you can. The others are blowing up, too.

Beginning with the eighth hole, Bobby settled down to reel off the rest of the round precisely in par. Even so, a 76 went on the board. Not so good—no.

And yet—Bobby was leading the field, with a single round to play. Cruickshank came in with a 78, and Hutchison, who had led them both at the halfway mark, collapsed with an 82.

After 54 holes, Bobby led with 220; Cruickshank was second with 223; and the Hutch was third, with 224. No one else was close enough to have a chance. The Inwood course had attended to that.

And now Bobby, leading the pack into the last round, made one more serious mistake. During the luncheon intermission—you may be sure it was no pie *à la mode*, but toast and tea that he ordered —he did a bit of figuring, the result of which was the conclusion that a 73 in the fourth round would be certain to win; and a 74 or a 75 most likely would be good enough. A 75, for example, would demand a par round of Cruickshank to tie him, while the Hutch would need a 71. He felt pretty sure that Cruickshank was the more formidable of the pursuers—Jock was unlikely to rally to a dangerous extent after that dreadful 82.

And, where he should have gone out for his last round intent on a cold, determined combat with Old Man Par, Bobby went out to do a round which he considered would be *good enough* to keep Cruickshank and the Hutch behind him.

He lost a stroke at the first hole, gained it back at the 520-yard fifth, reaching the green with two huge shots—and lost two strokes at the 223-yard seventh when his spoon drive, rolling along the edge of the fairway, struck a spectator's foot and hopped out of bounds. He was out in 39—not too bad; not too good. He never had been worse than par 35 coming in; and that, he believed, would do.

But coming in he started by holing a 20-foot putt for a birdie 3 at the tenth; he clipped another stroke from par with a birdie 4 at the 500-yard fourteenth; he got his par 3 after being bunkered from the tee on the short fifteenth—and then he saw a championship staring him in the face.

Par on the last three holes was 4-4-4. Twice he had done them 4-4-3. The third time it was 4-4-4. Once more, just in par, and he would do a 72 for the round—then Cruickshank would have to bring in a 69 to tie!

I sometimes think a championship is the cruelest crisis of all to face. Especially the first championship.

On three holes which he had never done worse than 4-4-4, Bobby finished 5-5-6.

The strain broke him. After a good drive at the sixteenth he pulled his iron second far out of bounds, and was very lucky to get down in one putt after a convenient mound had turned his next shot toward the flag. One stroke gone. He missed the seventeenth green with a long pitch. Another 5. Another stroke gone. And at the eighteenth, a hole of 425 yards guarded by a lagoon in front of the green, he played his second shot too carefully, taking a spoon against the light wind where he should have banged a hard iron over, and the ball was pulled off to the left under a chain strung about the twelfth tee.

I always have thought the delay here finished his collapse. The officials insisted on removing the chain, which was proper enough. Meanwhile Bobby sat on the turf and brooded over his wretched finish. Then he got up and popped the ball neatly into a bunker between him and the green. He finished that round with a terrible 6. He had lost four strokes to par on the last three holes. His total for the round was 76. For the tournament, 296. Cruickshank could tie him with a 73. A par 72 would win for him.

I went up to Bobby as he walked off the green. His face gave me such a shock that for a moment

I forgot what I meant to say. . . . His age seemed to have doubled in the last half hour.

"I think you're champion, Bobby," I said, after swallowing hard. "Cruickshank will never catch you."

Bobby was not one to kid himself. I've never forgotten what he said:

"Well, I didn't finish like a champion. I finished like a yellow dog."

And he went up to his room in the clubhouse, to wait for the jury to come in—the jury being Bobby Cruickshank.

I went over to see what was happening to the pursuit. I reached Cruickshank at the sixth green just in time to see him sink a big putt for a birdie 2. Starting there, he did seven consecutive holes in 23 strokes—two over 3's. He went to the sixteenth tee needing 4-4-4 to win by a stroke. The strain got him then, just as it had got Bobby more than an hour before. He took a 6 at the sixteenth and a par 4 at the seventeenth. That left him a birdie 3 at the last hole, to tie. He got it—a fine drive, a great iron, a seven-foot putt. . . . I can see him now, hitting that putt with the smooth precision of a machine, and fairly leaping after the ball, as if daring it not to drop. . . . It was one of the greatest holes ever played.

Cruickshank had finished with a 73. He and Bobby were tied for first place at 296. The Hutch was third, six strokes behind. Inwood had sorted them all out but two. They played off the tie at 18 holes the next afternoon.

In the annals of American sport there can be few combats as dramatic as that 18-hole play-off at stroke competition for the open championship of the United States. There was tension in the sultry air. A storm was brewing, and toward the middle of the round there was a recurrent flicker of lightning through the thunder-heads climbing sullenly up the western sky. And certainly there never was another play-off like that one—at fifteen of the eighteen holes, one or the other of the combatants gained a stroke; yet they were level as they stood on the last tee.

Here are the cards, with par of the course:

Par (out)	445	553	344 37
Jones	445	454	344—37
Cruickshank	534	543	445—37
Par (in)	443	453	444—35—72
Jones	552	455	454—39—76
Cruickshank	653	444	546—41—78

The cold figures show clearly the first-nine battle, level with par, and the collapse as they started the second nine, where, planting a steep pitch two feet from the flag at the twelfth hole, Bobby went two strokes ahead, only to lose them at the fourteenth and fifteenth.

It is Bobby's 200-yard iron shot to the water-guarded eighteenth green that is called the winning stroke. But a harder one to play, I think, was his drive from the seventh tee. And if the iron second at the eighteenth won the championship, the spoon shot at the seventh saved it.

Cruickshank, playing great golf after a wild drive from the first tee, was two strokes ahead of Bobby through the sixth hole—and Bobby was level with par. The seventh was the most dangerous one-shotter I ever saw—223 yards in length, down a narrow, lanelike fairway with out-of-bounds (a two-stroke penalty) on either side.

Cruickshank, with two strokes in hand, very properly played safe with an iron, short of the green; he was taking no chances of going out of bounds. Now Bobby had to decide whether to follow his adversary's example and play a safe iron shot or go for the green with a spoon. . . . He had been out of bounds there in the last round. One more at this juncture and he could kiss the championship good-by.

On the other hand, he needed to pick up a stroke. . . . He chose the spoon.

Bobby has told me that was the most difficult shot he ever played. But the ball reached and held the green, 25 feet from the flag. Cruickshank chipped ten feet short, missed the putt, and took a 4. Bobby got a stroke back.

Cruickshank missed a five-footer at the ninth, and they were square—out in par.

The bout became a scramble at the tenth, a 6 and a 5, with Bobby getting the 5; continued with two sorry 5's at the eleventh; Bobby gained another stroke by sticking his pitch dead at the short twelfth, and Cruickshank got them both back by his own great play at the long fourteenth and Bobby's bad play at the next. Cruickshank slipped at the sixteenth, and Bobby at the seventeenth, and they stood on the last tee, groggy and all square.

Cruickshank's drive was pulled far off line to a road back of a tree, so that he could only play a strong iron out short of the lagoon in front of the green. Bobby's drive was longer, sliced to the short rough, the ball lying on hard, dry turf. After Cruickshank had played short of the water Bobby had another decision to make—to go for the green or to play safe. But he does not in the least remem-

ber a decision, or anything about the shot. . . .
He asked me a bit shyly, next day on the train,
if he hesitated long over that shot, and if he
used a full or a three-quarters swing.

What he did was this:

He walked quickly to the ball, took one look
at it, one look at the pin, 200 yards away, with
the tiny lake in front of the green, pulled a No. 2
iron from the bag, and hit that shot as promptly
as ever he hit a golf ball in his life. . . . It went
away on a ruled line, straight for the flag. . . .
The applause came with a crash. But just before
it, Stewart Maiden, standing behind Bobby's
caddy, Luke Ross, swung his new straw hat high
in the air and brought it down to an utter ruin
on Luke's head. And Luke never knew it until
later. . . . Bobby says the first thing he really
remembers was Francis Ouimet holding him up
by one arm as the gallery charged past.

That was the winning shot. Bobby's ball almost
struck the pin, and stopped six feet beyond. Gallant little Cruickshank was done at last. His desperate attempt to pitch close to the flag sent the
ball rolling over into a bunker. His recovery was
20 feet past the pin. He missed the long putt.

Bobby Jones was open champion of the United

States. As Walter Hagen predicted two years before, at Columbia, he won the big one first.

Sitting beside him on the steps of the clubhouse, waiting for the cup presentation, I asked Bobby how he felt.

He looked at me a moment as if puzzled.

"Why," said he, "I don't care what happens now."

Something suddenly seemed to have been sticking in my throat a long time. . . . Perhaps as long as seven years.

CHAPTER XIV

THE SECOND BATTLE OF MERION

BOBBY and Stewart Maiden and I were in the humor for a bit of extravagance going home, so we had a drawing-room, and it was pretty deep with New York papers when we started, all with big headlines on the front page, about the new open champion. We read all the accounts, carefully. In a corner, at one end of the long seat, was the big cup. At the other end of the seat, in another corner, was Stewart. He never talked much, and he was talking less than usual. Indeed, I don't remember him talking at all. But his expression bore a marked resemblance to that of a cat which has recently come across a pan of cream uncovered. And Bobby and I didn't talk a great deal, either. I remember after one long pause Bobby reached under the seat and hauled out a battered traveling-bag and opened it and got out a green plush box. He opened the box and sat

188

staring at the big gold medal awarded by the United States Golf Association to the winner of a national championship.

"You know," he said, finally, "it's remarkably hard to get one of those things!"

I regarded this as an extremely conservative estimate.

The old home town put on the first of many tremendous welcomes, with a band and a parade which wound up at the Chamber of Commerce so the mayor and various prominent citizens could make speeches about Bobby, who was terribly embarrassed. He was more than embarrassed, too. When he faced that crowd, packing the auditorium to the doors, and the cheering started, Bobby —well, he had to turn away for a moment. It was the only time I ever saw him show a trace of emotion of that sort.

And now everybody, including the critics, had swung around to the conviction that winning championships was going to be pretty soft, for Bobby. Especially amateur championships. More especially the 1923 amateur championship, played two months after the open on the gigantic course of the Flossmoor Country Club, near Chicago. Bobby had broken through. The big one was in the bag. He had proved to everybody, including himself, that there existed no deficiency back of his belt buckle.

Reading the papers and the golf magazines before Flossmoor, you gained the impression that the amateur championship was as good as in the bag, also.

But it wasn't.

Bobby went wretchedly in practice, as at Inwood, but played well enough in the first qualifying round, on Saturday, and while many anxious competitors were out at the course practicing on Sunday, Bobby stopped at the hotel in bed, resting and reading Papini's *Life of Christ*.

He continued to play well on Monday, and at the conclusion of the second qualifying round he and Chick Evans were tied at 149 for the 36 holes, leading the field. This score was a good deal better than it may appear. The Flossmoor course was a tough layout, 7,000 yards around. Par was 74 in those days, and that also was the record.

And then, having tied for the medal, and being all set—as the critics fancied—to win his first national amateur championship, Bobby proceeded to lose to Max Marston in the second round, which was the earliest exit he had yet made from this competition.

In the first round Bobby played badly against

(*P. & A. Photos*)

BOBBY JONES AND JESS
SWEETSER

STEWART MAIDEN AND
BOBBY JONES

BOBBY JONES AND CHICK EVANS

T. B. Cochran, of Wichita Falls, Texas, who had got into the championship by a play-off, and had hard work beating him 2-1. In the next match, however, with Marston, Bobby seemed to have come on his game with a rush. Max was playing well himself, but as they stood on the seventeenth tee of the morning round the tall Philadelphian was 4 down, and Bobby needed two 4's for a 68, six better than par.

Indeed, during a short wait on the tee, Bobby heard somebody in the gallery say this, and for the first time in the match he began thinking about the score. The two finishing holes were long ones, close to 500 yards each, but it was not particularly difficult for a big hitter to get a birdie 4 at either. However, it was Marston who got the birdies. Bobby got a par 5 at each hole, and went in to luncheon only 2 up.

And, starting with those last two holes of the morning round, Marston traveled nineteen consecutive holes, to the end of that match, at the thirty-fifth green, just five strokes better than par. He beat Bobby, 2-1. And he went on to win the championship, defeating Jess Sweetser, the champion of 1922, on the thirty-eighth green of one of the greatest battles in history.

The night after the Marston match, Bobby and

I were talking about it at the hotel. Bobby was pretty blue. I asked him if he were going home before the tournament ended.

"Not I," he said. "They can lick me but they can't run me away!" Then he added: "I never expect to win an amateur championship, now. Somebody always goes crazy against me. Marston this time, and last year it was Jess Sweetser, and the year before that it was Willie Hunter. But I'm going to keep on playing in the blamed things, anyway. I'm going over to Merion next year, where I started, and I suppose somebody will lick me in the first round there. I've been licked in every round except the first."

"Yes," I suggested, "and you've won in every round—except the last. Maybe it will be that way, at Merion."

But he shook his head gloomily. Somebody always seemed to go crazy against him, in match-play.

And yet it was at Flossmoor that Bobby began learning his last big lesson from Old Man Par.

Chick Evans was beaten by Willie Hunter in the first round, and on Thursday he and Bobby decided to play off for the medal for which they were tied in the qualifying round. Chick started fast and gained two strokes in the first four holes.

But Bobby did not seem to be worrying. He was intensely concentrated. He did not appear to be paying the slightest attention to Chick or to Chick's play. He was paying no attention to anything except his own game. Walking off the fourteenth green, he passed so near me in the gallery that our elbows touched, and he looked right through me. Perhaps he was looking at Old Man Par. At any rate, he was giving the tough old fellow a tidy drubbing, with a new medal-play record of 72 for the huge course. And in beating par, Bobby rather took Chick Evans in his stride. Chick lost by four strokes, doing a 76.

"I wish I could play in a match like that," Bobby said afterward.

"So do I," was my reply. "Why don't you?"

It seemed there was a great difference in Bobby's attitude toward match-play, or hole competition, and medal play, or stroke competition, in which the total number of strokes for the round or the tournament is the factor. In match-play, Bobby confessed, he seemed to regard each hole as a detached and separate bout; if you take ten strokes on one hole, it's only one hole gone, and a neat little 3 may get it back at the next green. While if you take a 10 on one hole of a medal competition—good-by!

"In medal play," Bobby said, "I feel as if I'm at work on a definite structure, adding one par hole to another par hole, as if adding stories to a tall building. And if I blow a short putt here, why, I may get a long one down, later on. A matter of saving strokes, you might say."

There was nothing original in Bobby's decision, reached some time after Flossmoor, to try to play match golf as he did medal golf—to shoot against the card, the best he could, at every hole and, to put it somewhat impolitely, ignore his opponent as far as possible. Mr. John Ball, the great English amateur, carried this plan to the extent that he rarely looked to see where an opponent's ball went. And Mr. Ball was able to win eight British amateur championships at match-play; and in 1890 he won the British amateur and open the same season, which remained a record forty years, until Bobby did the same thing in 1930.

So Bobby decided to try out the plan of playing his best against par instead of matching shots with a human opponent; and his first opportunity in a match-play championship was at Merion, the year after Flossmoor. And there it worked very well indeed.

The first big event of 1924, however, was the national open at the Oakland Hills Country Club, near Detroit, where little Cyril Walker, a fragile appearing professional weighing only 120 pounds at the time, gave perhaps the most consistent performance, all things considered, that ever won our open championship, with rounds of 74-74-74-75—297 over a long course swept at all times by a hard wind. Cyril and Bobby were tied for the lead after the third round, and Bobby, playing an hour ahead of Walker, ran into a lot of varigated trouble, especially around the tenth hole, and finally had to do a birdie 4 against the wind at the long eighteenth to nose out Wild Bill Mehlhorn, who was then in the lead, having finished with a score of 301. Bobby's last round of 78, topped off with the birdie 4, left him with a total of 300, and that stood up until Walker, playing brilliantly and courageously under the pressure of knowing just what he had to do, came in with a 75 and a winning score of 297. Bobby was second, Mehlhorn was third, and little Bobby Cruickshank, who had fought such a gallant battle with Bobby the previous summer at Inwood, was tied at 303 for the next position with Walter Hagen and Macdonald Smith.

Sir Walter seemed rather subdued after this tournament, and somebody told me he had made a considerable wager on himself to finish ahead of

Bobby. Anyway, Hagen went on over to Britain and won the British open, which must have been a good deal of solace.

As for Bobby, he was so pleased with his birdie 4 at the finish, when he knew what he had to do to go ahead of Mehlhorn, that he really seemed very happy over the tournament.

"It took the taste of that 6 at Inwood out of my mouth," he explained. "For once in my life I had something hard to do under pressure, and *did* it."

Anyway, I suspect Bobby was not thinking too much about that 1924 championship, because he was going to be married less than a fortnight after it—Gene Sarazen also was to wed that June, and the golf-writers had a bit of gentle fun, speculating on the chances of one of the June brides receiving a big gold medal for a wedding present. But Gene, winner two years before, finished in a tie for seventeenth place with a score of 313. Bobby, you will observe, now was establishing that amazing habit of finishing either first or second in the biggest event in the Big Show. In the nine American open championships beginning with 1922 and ending with 1930, he was either first or second eight times, in great contrast to his leading rivals, who generally followed a championship by finishing fifteen or twenty positions below first place in the next one.

So Bobby went happily back to Atlanta and married his first sweetheart—the only sweetheart he ever had, I believe—Mary Malone, and they have lived happily ever after, to the date of this writing. They have three very fine children, Clara Malone Jones, Robert Tyre Jones III, and Mary Ellen Jones.

The famous Garden City Golf Club, on Long Island, was the scene of Bobby's next important competition, the Walker Cup match with Great Britain, and again Bobby was No. 2, with Max Marston, the amateur champion, as No. 1. Marston lost his singles match to Cyril Tolley, and Jess Sweetser, amateur champion of 1922, was beaten by the Hon. Michael Scott, and the Americans won the other six matches in singles, Bobby for his part defeating the gigantic Major Hezlet. In the foursomes, however, Bobby and W. C. Fownes, Jr., lost the only encounter for our side, being defeated, 1 up, by the Hon. Michael Scott and Robert Scott, Jr. This is the only instance in five international matches where Bobby had anything to do with losing a point for the Americans. Our team won this match, 9 to 3.

Then both sides moved over to Philadelphia and

played as individuals in the national amateur on the East Course of the Merion Cricket Club, where Bobby had made his bow in the Big Show just eight years before.

Things were different, now. The "chunky schoolboy" of fourteen, in his first major competition, had grown into a compact, powerful, seasoned veteran—a veteran competitor at twenty-two, about to try out at match-play a method that had carried him to the front rank in medal competition. It worked extraordinarily well, this playing calmly and steadily against par and letting the other fellows do what they could. Not one of them got really hot—not one of them went crazy and broke a record. I should say that the nearest thing to a real threat Bobby encountered in the Second Battle of Merion was from Ducky Corkran, after Bobby appeared to have the match perfectly in hand, being 5 up with five to play.

This was in the second round. Bobby had defeated W. J. Thompson, Canadian amateur, 6-5, in the first match and then he met Ducky, who had set a new record in the qualifying test with rounds of 67 and 75, for a total of 142, while Bobby was next with 144.

Bobby went serenely along against Corkran, just as if playing against the card in a medal competition, and gained consistently until they stood on the thirteenth tee of the afternoon round with Corkran 5 down. The hole is a puzzling little affair of 125 yards to a flat, table-top green completely surrounded by white sand, and when Bobby spanked his pitch up four feet from the flag I fancied they would shake hands there. But Corkran stuck a pitch six feet from the pin and they both holed for a deuce, so the match went on with Bobby dormie 5—that is, 5 up and five to play; another half would end it.

I stopped there to watch some other matches, being sure of the result of this one—and half an hour later I was shocked to hear that Jones and Corkran were still playing! That could mean only one thing—Ducky was winning every hole. I hustled over to the sixteenth green, where a huge gallery had assembled, just in time to see Corkran's ball come on the carpet from a great iron shot from the valley below. On came Bobby's ball, too. Each had a puzzling approach putt, and laid it close. Bobby holed for a par 4. They shook hands at last. The margin was 3-2. Corkran had won the fourteenth and fifteenth; and if he had won the sixteenth anything could have happened, for the two finishing holes at Merion are among the trickiest in the world.

But it was Old Man Par that Bobby was playing against, at the Second Battle of Merion. He didn't shoot precisely par at all times, of course. But he was plugging along, shooting *at* it. And what he managed to produce was just too good for the other boys. He beat Rudy Knepper 6-4 in the third round, and that brought him to the semi-finals with the man who had beaten him in that same round in 1920 at the Engineers Club—his dearest friend among the golfers, Francis Ouimet.

The night before that match I got back to our room at the Greenhill Farms Hotel and found Bobby in his pajamas, sitting on the side of his bed, and looking as if he were about to cry. What was the matter?

"I don't want to play Francis," he explained. "I'm going well, and his game is all shot to pieces, and I'm pretty sure I can beat him, and, darn it all—I don't *want* to beat him!"

This looked pretty serious. I asked Bobby if he wanted to win an amateur championship. He did. I asked him how his plan was coming on, to shoot at par and let the other fellows take care of themselves. He said it was working fine. All right.

"When you go out there on the first tee tomorrow morning," I told him, "you're not playing Francis Ouimet. You're playing the card of the

Merion Cricket Club's East Course. And so is Francis. The one who plays it closest will go into the finals on Saturday."

With a sorry 6 at the eighteenth hole next morning Bobby had a card of 73, and he was 8 up. The match ended on the eighth green that afternoon. Bobby had won, 11-10. They walked off that green with their arms about each other's shoulders, and if you had just arrived you'd have been sure that Bobby had lost and Francis had won.

George Von Elm was the other finalist, and their match next day was the beginning of a famous rivalry during years in which he and Bobby were regarded as the leading amateurs of America. Von Elm also was the last man to beat Bobby in a 36-hole match in a major championship, and the only man to win a 36-hole bout from him in formal competition in the last seven years of his career.

This, however, was not the time. Bobby in the final match of the 1924 championship continued to plug along steadily, undisturbed by George's winning the first hole, or by his own dismal 7 at the long fourth. Bobby was 2 up at the turn and 4 up at the end of the morning round. He went away fast in the afternoon—toast and tea for luncheon, not pie *à la mode*—and the match ended at the tenth green, 9-8.

Bobby long afterward confessed to a reflection which may appear a bit rude, when they presented the cup and the gold medal to him. You know he had been trying to win this championship for eight years. And yet, as he stood there, listening to a fine speech about himself and his golf, he thought:

"Now, I've won the blamed thing—and I didn't do anything, either!"

Bobby meant, of course, that he hadn't done anything more than usual—this time none of the fellows went crazy against him.

It may be merely a coincidence, but after Bobby made up his mind to play against Old Man Par in his matches, nobody ever did go crazy against him again, as Sweetser at Brookline, and Marston at Flossmoor.

CHAPTER XV

AMBITION, AND SOME LICKINGS

TO THE end of his competitive golfing career, the dashing D'Artagnan would occasionally assert himself under the iron mask and the cool precision that, after the Second Battle of Merion, gained for Bobby Jones the apt though not altogether fitting sobriquet, the Mechanical Man of Golf. There was that ultra-delicate and over-bold niblick pitch over the deep bunker guarding the fourteenth green at Pebble Beach, which cost him the first-round match with Johnny Goodman, in the national amateur of 1929. And there was the similar pitch for the last green of the second play-off in the national open at Worcester, in 1925. Each of these shots was aimed at a human opponent—not at Old Man Par. And each resulted fatally.

Through one of the most utterly eccentric struggles in golfing history, Bobby Jones and Willie Macfarlane, the tall, slender, bespectacled

professional from Oak Ridge, had worked themselves into a tie at 291 for first place in the national open championship of 1925 at the Worcester Country Club, near Boston. Bobby had started
with a terrible 77, in which was involved almost every mistake a first-rank golfer can make,
and in which also was included a penalty stroke,
which he called on himself, when his ball, in long
grass on a steep bank at the side of the eleventh
green, rolled a couple of inches as he took his
stance and prepared to play the shot.

There has been a lot said and written concerning this penalty—entirely too much, Bobby always
considered. Once when I had written an inter-
view with him for the Associated Press, after he
became the first world champion of golf, and had
mentioned this circumstance, Bobby was out-
raged.

"You'd as well praise me for not breaking into
banks," he said. "There is only one way to play
this game."

You see, nobody but Bobby believed he had
caused the ball to move—which under the rules
constitutes a stroke—and the championship committee had questioned him and several others, before posting his score. The others all said they
did not believe Bobby had caused the ball to move.

Mr. Fownes, vice-president of the U. S. G. A., turned to Bobby again.

"Well, Bobby," he said, "it seems a matter for you to decide. Do you think you caused that ball to move?"

"I *know* I did," was the reply.

And the score went on the board, 77 instead of 76.

Since at the end of the fourth round Bobby and Willie Macfarlane were tied for the lead, a good many writers took the somewhat simple-minded position that that penalty stroke had cost Bobby the championship, as he lost in the play-off. But that is mere speculation. If Bobby had not lost the stroke there, he might have lost it somewhere else—and conceivably several others. A golf championship, especially at medal play, is pretty much an entity, it seems, and it is idle to speculate on what the result would have been had one stroke or one hole been altered.

However, the 77 put Bobby in thirty-sixth place for the first day's play, and one newspaper that evening spread this banner across its front page:

"Jones Out of National Open."

Like the report of Mark Twain's death, this was a great exaggeration.

Bobby came back with a 70 in the second round,

but this left him six strokes away from the lead at the halfway post, as Macfarlane had clicked off a miraculous 31 for the last nine holes of his second round, for a 67, and his total now was 141, in a tie with Leo Diegel, who had done a 68 to go with his 73 of Round 1.

Saturday morning, Bobby did another 70 in the third round, but gained only two strokes on Willie, who had done that last nine once more in startling fashion—a 32 after a dismal 40 going out. Willie's total was 213 for three rounds. Johnny Farrell with a 69 slipped into second place with 214; Francis Ouimet was next with 216, and Bobby was 217.

Again came the last-round blow-off, and Bobby, remembering Inverness and Inwood, stuck to an apparently hopeless task, did a 74—and went into a tie for first place with Macfarlane, who required 78 for the last round. Diegel seemed to be winning twice, in that round. He went out in 34, and suddenly was in front. But he came back in 44, where a simple 38 would have won for him, and was well down the list. Francis Ouimet and Johnny Farrell were tied for third place, at 292, and Hagen and Sarazen tied at 293 for the next position.

In those days, the play-off of a tie in the national open was at 18 holes, and at the end of the

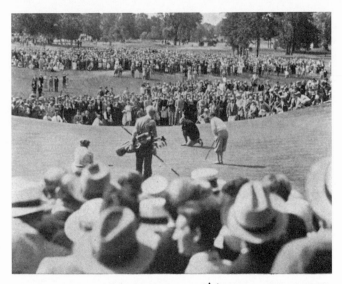

THE MOST IMPORTANT STROKE IN JONES'S CAREER—THE TWELVE-
FOOT PUTT, NATIONAL OPEN—WINGED FOOT, 1929

JONES VS. TOLLEY, THE EIGHTEENTH HOLE, BRITISH AMATEUR
—ST. ANDREWS, 1930

round next morning, Bobby and Willie MacFarlane were still tied, at 75 strokes. Willie had
rather outplayed the great amateur, who had
saved himself what looked like a loss of two
strokes by holing a short pitch at the fourteenth
hole for a birdie 3 after two bad shots had made
a 5 most probable. Willie missed a six-foot putt
at the last green that would have settled the championship right there, and I couldn't help feeling
that Bobby, younger and stronger, and twice
saved by fortune in the morning, would get him
in the afternoon.

For nine holes there seemed no doubt about it.
Willie stuck with him the first three, and then
Bobby, playing exactly level with par, picked up
four strokes by the time they reached the turn.
He was out in par 35. Willie required 39. I was
feeling sorry for Willie. The sympathy was vastly
misplaced. I had forgotten his penchant for scoring on that last nine.

Willie started home with a 2 and at the next
one-shotter holed a 20-foot putt for another 2,
and was only one stroke behind. Bobby set out
to reach the fifteenth green, 555 yards from the
tee, with a great drive and second—and was
bunkered for his boldness, while Willie, playing

conservatively for a par 5, gained back the last stroke of the deficit.

They halved the sixteenth. Going to the seventeenth, Bobby walked over to me, waiting for Willie to play his second shot at the other side of the fairway.

"This thing's getting funny," he said. "Still tied—after one hundred and six holes!"

"Looks like a third play-off," I suggested.

His face hardened a bit.

"No," he said, "there won't be another play-off. I'll settle it one way or another, in this round."

He did. They halved the seventeenth, and were still tied. The eighteenth is a drive-and-pitch affair of 335 yards, uphill, to a small, shelf-like green notched into a hillside, with a steep bank and a deep bunker across the front. The pin was very near this edge.

Bobby hit a great drive, far in front of Macfarlane, who played a safe, conservative pitch to the back of the green, some 40 feet past the flag.

Then Bobby, as he had said, settled the play-off. It was not the Mechanical Man of Golf, swinging a mashie-niblick, so much as the young D'Artagnan, staking all on a brilliant thrust. The shot was aimed to pitch a mere foot beyond the front edge of the shelf, so the ball might trickle up close to the flag for a birdie 3.

It missed the edge—by four inches. The ball hung a breathless instant; then rolled back into the deep bunker. The blast left a putt of eight feet. Macfarlane, playing with grand nerve, sent his long approach putt up stone dead. Bobby missed. After one hundred and eight holes, Macfarlane was one stroke ahead. He was open champion. Bobby was runner-up—the third time in four years.

But he was not to complete the year 1925 without a national title. The amateur championship, played at Oakmont—where Davy Herron had beaten him in the final round of 1919—came along the first week in September, and the Association tried an experiment which never has been repeated —the qualification of sixteen competitors instead of thirty-two. This permitted the entire tournament to be played in six days, in place of starting it on the Saturday of one week and running it through the next week. But so many popular players were left out of the sixteen that the plan was changed the following year; two 18-hole matches were substituted for the first 36-hole bout; and the play was confined to six days, with thirty-two qualifiers.

Watts Gunn, a *protégé* of Bobby's, was the picturesque figure at Oakmont in 1925. His father, Judge Will Gunn of Atlanta, did not consider Watts a sufficiently good golfer to enter the national amateur; but Bobby out-talked the Judge and gained a promise that Watts might compete.

The new Atlanta entry justified Bobby's good opinion—almost too emphatically. He qualified easily, defeated Vincent Bradford in the first round with a performance that stands as a world record for major championship match-play—he won fifteen consecutive holes against the hapless West Pennsylvania champion; gave Jess Sweetser, conqueror of Bobby in 1922, the worst beating Jess ever received in a major competition; and met Bobby, his guide, philosopher and friend, in the final match.

And after the first eleven holes had been played, Bobby was a stroke better than par on that tremendous Oakmont course—and was 1 down. Also, he was up to his neck in a bunker at the right of the twelfth green, the long "Ghost Hole" at Oakmont; and Watts was neatly on the putting surface, sure for a par 5.

"I couldn't help thinking," Bobby said, whimsically, long afterward, "of the eloquent speech I made to Judge Gunn, begging him to send Watts to that championship. And here he was taking it away from me! I felt then, and I feel now, that if I hadn't got that ball out and canned a good putt for a half, I'd never have collared Watts. He was playing inspirational golf of the most devastating kind."

However, Bobby *did* get that ball out of the bunker, and he *did* hole a ten-foot putt for a half. And then, as the saying is, he turned on the heat. In the next eight holes of that match he did five 3's. And this was too much for the gallant Watts. He never ceased fighting, but Bobby ended the battle at the eleventh green of the afternoon round, 8-7.

It was after this tournament that Bobby told me, in strict confidence at the time, of his ambition in competitive golf.

"If I could be national champion of the United States six years in succession, either open or amateur," he said, "then I'd feel that I could hang up the old clubs."

Of course it didn't seem possible, though he had accomplished half the ambition. And we didn't even speak of it again, for years. It seemed the dream of a D'Artagnan, who, you remember, was a Gascon. Yet in the end, when he hung up the clubs, it was eight years in succession instead of six; and there were four British championships, and two world championships, in the bag as well.

The first of these latter was achieved in 1926, the year after Oakmont, and a year which began, oddly enough, with the soundest thrashing Bobby Jones ever received in a golf competition of any kind.

Bobby was spending the winter at Sarasota, Florida, where he was in business at the time, and he was playing a lot of golf, notably with Tommy Armour, now a professional, as his partner against pairs of some of the best professionals in America, wintering in Florida. As I recall it, Bobby and Tommy won a series of seven consecutive four-ball matches, including one bout with Walter Hagen and Gil Nicholls, who were over at Pasadena. Walter was national professional champion at the time; Bobby was national amateur champion; they liked to play against each other; and a 72-hole match was arranged, the first half at Bobby's course at Sarasota, and the second half at Walter's Pasadena course.

I do not recall finer match-golf than Walter Hagen displayed straight through that engagement. Bobby's iron play was a bit off, certainly; I think this encounter impressed him with the need of doing something about it. But he was

playing very well—and he was 8 down at the end
of the first 36 holes; and he was beaten 12-11 in
the finish at the Pasadena Club.

I rather more than suspect that in this match
Bobby abandoned his idea of competition against
par to match strokes with his human opponent—
and Walter Hagen, with his astounding talent
for recovery and his superb play about the greens,
was the last opponent in the world against whom
to adopt this policy. Be that as it may, I think
Bobby was in for a great beating, no matter what
policy he adopted. Hagen was better than par all
through the match; he outplayed Bobby at every
material point; and he deserved amply to win.

So it was a somewhat chastened American amateur champion who set sail later that spring with
the Walker Cup team, to play in the international
match at St. Andrews, and in the British amateur
championship at Muirfield, which came first.
Watts Gunn's performance at Oakmont the previous year had earned him a place on the Walker
Cup team, and he and Bobby planned also to stay
over and play in the British open, at Lytham and
St. Anne's, up Liverpool way.

But even before the British amateur Bobby had
got homesick to a degree that caused him to aban-
don the idea of staying over for the British open.

He had left behind him his wife and a little daughter, a year old, and the rest of his family; and soon after reaching Britain he had booked a return passage on the *Aquitania* with other members of the Walker Cup team who were sailing two days after that match.

Fate took a hand in these arrangements later, as you will see.

In the British amateur, Bobby went well enough in the opening matches, and by the fifth round, against Robert Harris, then British amateur champion, he was at the very top of his game. He began by holing a run-up approach of twenty-five yards for a 3 at the first hole; he went out in 35 against a par of 38; and he won nine of the twelve holes the match lasted. The British champion was beaten 8-6.

And the next morning an unknown young Scot named Andrew Jamieson found his way into front-page stories all over the world, when he stopped the American champion 4-3 in a match in which Jamieson was a stroke better than par and Bobby three strokes over.

This left Jess Sweetser the only American, and Jess survived to the end, the first American-born golfer to win the British amateur championship. Jamieson was beaten in the next round by Simpson, another Scot, and Sweetser, after two terrific battles with Francis Ouimet and the Hon. W. G. Brownlow, had no great difficulty in the final match with Simpson, at 36 holes.

Bobby was pretty blue after his defeat in the British amateur. More than ever he wanted to go home. And—this is where fate took a hand—if he had won the British amateur, it is certain that he would have gone home after the Walker Cup match, with the rest of his team-mates. And with him would have gone, along with the great cup, the chance of a world championship that year.

For Bobby decided not to sail on the *Aquitania* on June 5.

"It wouldn't be sporting," he said. "It would look as if I were sulking because I didn't win the amateur."

He had little enough hope of winning the British open. No amateur had won it since Harold Hilton, in 1897, five years before Bobby was born. But Bobby remembered, too, that he hadn't behaved any too well in the British open five years before; and, after all, he had said he was going to play at St. Anne's.

"And I'll go through with it," he decided.

But first there was the Walker Cup match at St. Andrews. And there Bobby played so well that he began to get a bit excited over the prospect of competition in the British open—though of course he said nothing about that. In the singles, he defeated Cyril Tolley 12-11, and in the foursomes he and Watts Gunn defeated Tolley and Andrew Jamieson 4-3. The big match was fearfully close. The Americans won three out of four bouts in the foursomes, unexpectedly, and even more unexpectedly lost four of the eight matches at singles, and halved another, so it really was the gallant play of George Von Elm against Major Hazlet, late in the day, that saved a narrow victory for our side. The best George could do was to get a draw with the gigantic Major; but that gave the Americans 6½ points to 5½ in one of the closest battles in the history of the match.

Bobby now was very serious about the British open. The rest of the team sailed away on the *Aquitania*, except for Watts Gunn and Roland Mackenzie and George Von Elm, who also were to play at St. Anne's, and Bobby went over to that course to get in some practice before the qualifying rounds, which he was to play with the southern section, at Sunningdale, near London.

I did not accompany him to St. Anne's. I chaperoned Watts Gunn and Roland Mackenzie on their first expedition to Paris, and we had a very wonderful time.

Bobby played only moderately well, in practice at St. Anne's. But when he went down to Sunningdale it was another story.

CHAPTER XVI

WORLD CHAMPION

THE finest round of golf Bobby Jones ever played was over the Old Course (there is a New Course now) of the Sunningdale Golf Club, in Surrey, not far from London; his first of two rounds, qualifying for the British open championship of 1926. Mr. Bernard Darwin said at the time it was the finest round ever played in Britain. So far as I know, and assuredly so far as I have observed, there never was one to compare with it in America. There have been lower-scoring rounds—Bobby has scored better himself—though I do not recall a card as good connected with a major championship at medal play. The point is, this score of 66 was registered by almost perfect golf, played with a precision and a freedom from error never attained before or since by the greatest precisionist of them all.

I said "almost" perfect golf. There was a single

error in the round. At the thirteenth hole, a one-
shotter of 175 yards, Bobby's iron permitted the
ball to trickle a yard too far on the fast green; it
rolled into a shallow pot-bunker, from which he
chipped, and holed the putt for a par 3. The mistake did not cost him anything—the customary
rating of a mistake. But it was the single flaw in
what Mr. Darwin characterized—rather affec-
tionately, I fancied—as a "brilliantly dull" round.

Bobby loved the Sunningdale course as soon as
he played it. In practice before the qualifying test
he scored two rounds of 66 against a par of 72.
The course record was 70 for competitive play.
Bobby had picked up a beautifully modeled driver
from Jack White, then the Sunningdale professional, and he seemed to have found a sudden
inspiration in it.

Old Jack told me at the United States open
championship of 1929 that he had named the
driver Jeannie Deans.

"Anything in Scotland that is beloved or spe-
cially heroic," Jack explained, "is 'Jeannie Deans,'
after the beloved heroine of that name."

Bobby never played with any other driver in
competition thereafter. And he won ten major
championships with Jeannie Deans.

The Sunningdale record, then, was 70 when the

southern section started the qualifying rounds there in June, 1926. Archie Compston, the tall English professional, promptly lowered it, with a fine 69 early in the day. At mid-afternoon, Bobby started, playing, oddly enough, with a little English professional also named Jones. And he came in with a card of 66, compiled in this singularly symmetrical fashion:

He played the first nine in 33, and the last nine in 33. He had 33 putts and 33 other shots. He had neither a 2 nor a 5—six 3's and twelve 4's. He holed only one long putt, of 25 feet, and to pay for it he missed two putts of five feet, each for a birdie. He had twelve pars and six birdies. The card, with par, was as follows:

```
Par (out) ......  554  344  434—36
Jones ..........  444  334  434—33

Par (in) .......  544  353  444—36—72
Jones ..........  434  343  444—33—66
```

And Sunningdale was a long course, and one of the finest inland layouts in England.

That evening, after dinner at the little Wheatsheaf Hotel at Virginia Water, Bobby was a bit nervous and, as the saying is, keyed up. He wasn't sleepy. And he and George Von Elm and Archie Compston and I set out for a walk in the cool, long English twilight, and we wound up walking around the lake. We didn't know when we started that it was ten miles. We got in just at midnight. Bobby slept pretty well, after that stroll, and next day he did a 68 to go with his 66, for a new record in the qualifying rounds of the British open.

I was worried, and so was Bobby. The Sunningdale performance meant that he had come on his game a week too soon. The place for such rounds was in the championship proper—only one never seems to get them there. He was gratified by the improvement in his iron play, as shown at Sunningdale, which necessitated a lot of it; as I recall it, Bobby used a mashie twice and a mashie-niblick once for approach shots in the 36 holes; as suggested, Sunningdale was a long course. Most of his shots to the green were good bangs with the irons, sometimes a spoon, and occasionally a brassie. Sunningdale was no drive-and-pitch affair, such as phenomenally low scores usually are made on.

But we both realized that Bobby had become too good too soon. And I know he was nervous enough when the Big Show began at St. Anne's over a fine, sunny, and always wind-swept course.

To quote Mr. Darwin again, Bobby won that championship without ever being on his game.

It was a triumph of determination and the cool resourcefulness of experience, rather than the invincible precision of Sunningdale. There also was a single shot, close to the finish, which was the turning point between victory and defeat.

Bobby's scores look regular enough: 72-72-73-74—291. And the total was as low as ever had been made in the British open, at that time. But he had to fight grimly for every score, with never an easy round where the ball was rolling for him.

In his first round, of 72, he was out in 37 and to come home in 35 he used only a single putt at each of the last four greens, holing two of six feet, one of ten, and the last one of twenty. And that sort of thing is as far removed as possible from golf of the Sunningdale brand.

Walter Hagen started with a rush and with a card of 68 was in front of the field after the first round. Bobby's second 72 passed him, however, and put the amateur in a tie for first place with Wild Bill Mehlhorn.

For the third and fourth rounds, Bobby was paired with another American, Al Watrous, a young professional, who was two strokes behind him as they started. In the morning round, Watrous did a fine 69 to Bobby's 73, and when they went up to our room at the Majestic Hotel for a bite of luncheon and a rest between rounds, Al was leading the field with a total of 215, and Bobby was second, with 217.

The situation now was as cruel as possible, for the two leaders. Playing together, they could not help playing against each other; they knew well enough that to win that championship they had to beat each other—and they knew just as well that, with Walter Hagen and George Von Elm on their heels, and Hagen in particular playing more than an hour behind them, any slipping on their part during their personal duel would give the great Haig the chance he loved—a driving finish to win.

I always liked the way Bobby advised his young professional rival to leave the scoreboard and go back with him to the hotel between rounds. The Haig was starting late, and the worst possible thing a leading competitor can do is to hang about, watching and worrying, when he still has a round to play. The boys went up to our room, and I pulled their shoes off and they lay down on the twin beds while I ordered their frugal luncheon. I pulled down the shades, and I heard Bobby tell Al for goodness' sake not to take a nap. That is almost certainly fatal, between rounds. And as they started back to the club, to begin their final round, I heard Bobby say:

"Remember, Al, the winner and the runner-up are in this pair!"

It is not only heroes of fiction who can be courtly and sportsmanlike. Golf has supplied its counterparts of Saladin and Cœur de Lion.

That last round, Bobby has said, was a nightmare. He was playing golf in his best vein at last—up to the green. And there the putts simply would not fall. In the sweeping wind he put his back into the big shots, hitting the ball farther and farther; he planted his approaches closer and closer to the flag—and missed the putts. Three times he got back one of the two strokes by which Watrous led him, and three times he lost it again. And at the fourteenth tee Watrous still led him by two strokes, and, of course, if he couldn't collar Al, it made no difference what Von Elm and the Haig might do.

At the last, it was Old Man Par who collared Watrous, and then pulled him back. Bobby played the last five holes 4-3-4-4-4, and that is cold, level par; no better. But the strain that finally was sending Bobby's ball into the hole was switching Al's away. He took three putts at the fourteenth, three at the fifteenth, and three at the seventeenth. And it was at this hole the winning stroke was delivered in the British open championship of 1926.

Permit me to quote again from Mr. Darwin, in *Green Memories*:

St. Anne's had, to be sure, one supremely exciting moment. Bobby and Watrous, his most dangerous competitor, were drawn to play together, as Vardon and Taylor had been at Prestwick in 1914. They had almost played each other to a standstill, and when they stood all square with two holes to play, it was by no means certain that either of them would win. Hagen was away in the distance, playing his last round, and he had something more than an outside chance. Still, either Bobby or Watrous was the likeliest winner, and after the tee shots to the seventeenth it seemed considerable odds on Watrous. He had hit a perfect shot and Bobby had hooked into a waste of sand on the left. I was walking with Mr. Fownes at the time and he was talking of all it would be worth to Watrous to win the British championship. Looking at his ball where it lay in the middle of the fairway, within a comfortable iron shot of the green, he said, "Yes, he'll have that shot for 100,000 dollars."

At that very moment Bobby shattered these bright visions by one of the most melodramatic shots ever played. True, he was lucky to get a good lie; but still he was on sand, he must have been 170 yards from the hole with the green partially hidden from him and all manner of difficulties lurking as they lurk at every hole at St. Anne's, and he hit that ball as clean as a whistle right up to the green, so that he had, humanly speaking, a certain 4. No

225

wonder that poor Watrous faltered, played rather a weak second to the outskirts of the green and took three more to get down. He took 5 at the last hole also, and Bobby beat him by two strokes. It had been a knock-out blow.

After that round, and when Hagen and Von Elm had failed to close the gap and were tied for third place, two strokes back of Al Watrous, a little Scottish golf-writer, Charlie Macfarlane—the same Charlie Macfarlane who beat Chick Evans in so spectacular a fashion in the British amateur of 1914—came to me with tears rolling down his face.

"O. B.," he said, "do you think Bobby would give me the club he made that shot with—the greatest shot in the history of British golf?"

As you may fancy, I was in a superbly generous humor.

"I'm sure he will, Charlie," I told him. "And I'll just go and get it for you now."

It was a favorite mashie-iron of Bobby's, but when I told him about it he couldn't be very grumpy. He did say, however, that it seemed to be a case of losing championships or pet clubs.

So Bobby's name went on the quaint, old-fashioned, beautiful silver pitcher emblematic of the British open championship, the first amateur's name since Harold Hilton, in 1897, five years before Bobby was born—along with the names of the Great Triumvirate, Vardon and Taylor and Braid, and the other heroes of more than half a century of competition. . . . Everybody gets sort of worked up and sentimental at an open championship. I remember Jack MacIntyre, the Scottish caddy who had carried Bobby's clubs at Muirfield and St. Andrews, and had in some way got over to St. Anne's, to carry for him in the open. Jack was waiting at the foot of the elevator to tell Bobby good-by, as we set out for Liverpool to take the night train for London. He stepped up to Bobby and held out his hand and tried to say something, but couldn't.

Bobby put an arm about Jack's shoulders.

"Jack, old man," he said, not very steadily, "I'd never have done it without you."

And Jack sat right down on the floor of that hotel lobby and began to sob like a small child.

As we got on the boat train at London next morning, Bobby said:

"When I see that old *Aquitania*, I'm going to pick it right up in my arms and hug it!"

At New York. . . . Well, it was one of those welcomes that New York above all cities can give: the steamer *Macom* with the greeting party to take the hero off at Quarantine; the bands resounding along the deep canyon of Broadway; the ticker tape coming down in spiraling clouds. . . . Mrs. Bobby was there, and Bobby's father and mother and grandfather and grandmother, and a hundred more of the home folks from Atlanta. . . . The band played "Valencia" up Broadway. I've never heard it since without my throat getting tight.

Bobby went on from New York to Columbus, for the United States open championship at the Scioto Country Club, starting just two weeks after the British open ended. Mary and his parents went on with him, and I think he had very little idea of winning. A number of great professionals had tried to win the British and the American open the same season, but no one had succeeded. Bobby was pretty well shot out, from St. Anne's; he was thoroughly stale, he was still on sea-legs, and after two rounds it seemed he didn't have a chance.

He went away fast in the first round with a 70 against a par of 72—the only time in the tournament he got a par 3 at the 140-yard ninth, which was a sort of Jonah hole for him there. Mehlhorn led the field with a 68, but he was the only man ahead of Bobby. After the second round there were plenty ahead of him. It was another of those

228

struggles in which nothing would go right; he called another penalty on himself when his ball moved on the fifteenth green as he addressed it— he set the putter-blade down in front, to get the line, and the wind evidently had been holding the ball in place, for it immediately rolled forward. And at the last hole he played recklessly and foolishly, for a veteran of his experience and knowledge. His drive was shoved out to the very deep rough and he tried to extract it with a No. 2 iron, and save a chance for a birdie 4 by getting near the green. The shot didn't go anywhere, and he wound up with a horrid 7 and a card of 79, equaling the worst score he ever returned in a national open.

Bobby was now six strokes back of Mehlhorn, who was leading the pack with 143, and four strokes behind Joe Turnesa, who assumed the lead in the third round. He was showing signs of the long strain. He was sick at his stomach, Saturday morning, and instead of trying any breakfast he went past a doctor's office and got something designed to settle that refractory member, with indifferent results.

Bobby says that his winning of the national open of 1926 was a pure, unadulterated accident.

But I agree with Big Bob, who greeted his son in the locker-room when Bobby came in from his fourth round, leading the field, but with two men out who had a fair chance to catch him.

Big Bob put both hands on his son's shoulders.

"Son," he said, "the winning of this championship doesn't matter now. What *does* matter is that you finished this day, of all days, with a score of absolute par. Son, I congratulate you on the greatest exhibition of gameness I have ever seen."

And Bobby said, simply, "Thank you, dad," and went back to the hotel to pack up, not knowing whether he had won or not.

He had played a fine round that morning, a 71, but Turnesa with a 72 had gone to the front and was leading, with 217, Bill Mehlhorn being second with 219. Bobby was third, at 220.

Turnesa started twenty minutes before Bobby in the final round. And hole for hole they scored exactly the same, until the short ninth—Bobby's *bête noir*. There Joe did a par 3 and Bobby took a 4. He was four strokes down with nine holes to play.

Each did a 4 at the tenth, and at the eleventh. Four strokes down, and seven holes to play. At the huge twelfth, nearly 600 yards, the break began. Turnesa, without any very bad play, slipped to a

6. Bobby stuck a short pitch a dozen feet from the flag and holed the putt for a birdie 4. Two strokes down now. As he went to the thirteenth tee some one told him Joe had taken a 5 there—a stroke over par. Bobby's 4 cut the lead to one stroke. Joe barely missed the greens at the fourteenth and seventeenth, par 3 holes—the first a big spoon-shot. Bobby was square, then a stroke ahead. Joe rallied for a last stand with a great birdie 4 at the 480-yard finishing hole. His total score went on the board, 294. It left Bobby a par 5 to tie him; a birdie 4 to go ahead.

That drive from the seventy-second tee at Scioto in the open championship of 1926 was not the longest Bobby ever hit in competition. Ten years before, in his lusty, carefree boyhood, in the national amateur championship at Merion, he had walloped a drive from the eighth tee that rolled across the green and into the bunker beyond. And that hole was then, and is today, 350 yards in length.

But I am sure that Bobby never hit a bigger drive in a pinch than that one at the very end of 72 holes of murderous strain, at the end of a day without a morsel of food, at the end of 36 holes in which he needed a birdie 4 to stay level with Old Man Par—and to go ahead of Joe Turnesa.

There was a sweeping cross-wind from the right, not at all the kind to help the range of a shot, but rather calculated to swing far off line a ball hit with anything less than absolute accuracy. . . . Bobby hit that last drive 310 yards. His second shot was a firm half-stroke with a mashie-iron, on a hole 480 yards in length. His knees were shaking so he could hardly stand as he played that shot, and they seemed buckling under him as he walked after it. The ball was twenty feet past the flag. He nearly holed a 3. His putt for the first golfing championship of the world was less than six inches.

CHAPTER XVII

THE SECOND BATTLE OF ST. ANDREWS

BOBBY came to the national amateur championship of 1926 with a great opportunity to equal one record and establish a number of others. By winning this tournament he could match Chick Evans's achievement of capturing the open and the amateur titles of the United States in the same season. And he could make it three amateur championships in a row, which never had been done—and, to this writing, has not been done yet. Also he could be the only competitor who had won the British open and the United States amateur in the same season, just as he already was the only American amateur who had ever won the British open at all.

At the Baltusrol Golf Club, in New Jersey, it appeared for five days that Bobby was likely to realize these various ambitions. He started by winning the medal in the qualifying round with a score of 143, a stroke better than the very tough par of the course, and a stroke worse than the record. The plan of the championship now had been altered so that the qualifying rounds were played Monday and Tuesday, two matches at 18 holes on Wednesday, and a match at 36 holes on Thursday, Friday and Saturday. Recalling Bobby's misadventures in the 18-hole bouts of the British amateur, the general opinion was that if Bobby could get by the "sudden death" battles on Wednesday he would win the championship.

Dicky Jones gave him a hard fight in the first match, leading at the tenth hole, but Bobby finally got him, though he had to finish the match with a birdie 4 at the long eighteenth to hold an advantage of 1 up.

Bill Reekie was not so obstinate in the afternoon, and Bobby, safely past the 18-hole bouts, went into the third round next day with Chick Evans—their first meeting at match-play since Evans had defeated him in 1920 in the western amateur championship.

This was a grim battle all the way, until Evans finally cracked going into the last nine, and Bobby won, 3-2. The match, I think, took a lot out of him, as did also his encounter with Francis Ouimet in the semi-final round. Bobby was 3 up at the end of the morning play, and some idea of the severity of the match is gained from the fact that in the afternoon Bobby played the first nine holes in 33 and gained only one hole. The winning margin was 5-4.

Meanwhile, George Von Elm, after a real struggle in the qualifying round and an extra-hole finish with Ellsworth Augustus in the opening match, was going steadily along in the other bracket, playing better and better—coming on his game just at the right time. He defeated Watts Gunn, the other Atlanta entry, 8-7, in the third round, while Bobby was engaged in the battle with Evans, and beat George Dawson 11-10 in the semi-finals. And then he and Bobby were in a match for the third time in three years.

Some of the critics were saying the tournament now was in the bag for Bobby.

"He's got George's number," they said. They were recalling that Bobby had beaten George 9-8 at Merion and 7-6 at Oakmont.

Bobby did not share this opinion.

"Nobody is going to keep on beating a golfer as good as George Von Elm," he said to me at the hotel, the morning before the match.

And so it turned out, in one of the hardest and best matches ever played in the American amateur. George was just at the peak of his game; Bobby seemed just over the peak of his. Bobby finished the 35 holes of the bout with a card a stroke above par. George, with two stymies against him, was a stroke better than par. His margin was 2-1.

So Bobby had to forego the various records for a time—we fancied it probably would be forever. For how could there be a bigger year than 1926?

Still, 1927 started auspiciously with a big open tournament at Bobby's home course, East Lake; the southern open, played there for the first time since 1920, when Bobby was runner-up to Douglas Edgar. Most of the crack American professionals were entered; a really fine field including Hagen and Farrell and Diegel and Cruickshank and Long Jim Barnes, who had won the southern open there in 1919; and Willie Macfarlane, and a lot of others. The purse, of $12,000, attracted plenty of the best professional talent.

Bobby started with a modest round of 72 and was in a tie for second place, with Emmett French leading the field with a 71. Then he broke away with a 66, the best score he had made in serious competition, always excepting the famous score at Sunningdale. That settled the championship. Bobby was five strokes in the lead after that round, and with cards of 71 and 72 finished with a score of 281, eight strokes ahead of Johnny Farrell and John Golden, who tied for first money.

This brilliant display, against a majority of the men he would find in the national open the following June at Oakmont, was regarded as an indication that Bobby would be extremely hard to beat for the second consecutive open championship. He liked the huge course, too, and had played grand golf in winning the amateur there in 1925. And so, when he finished the competition of 1927 with the worst score and the lowest position he had ever registered in the national open championship, a lot of people said he had been over-confident.

This was not in the least true. When he went to Oakmont he was just out of Emory University, where he had been studying law; he had had very little opportunity for practice; and, in short, he was playing wretchedly. His performance in the southern open really meant nothing. It was at the course on which he was brought up; as he used to say, he should be able to kick the ball around it in par.

Everybody scored badly at Oakmont. Tommy Armour finally holed a ten-foot putt for a 3 at the last green to tie Harry Cooper for first place at 301, and defeated him in the play-off. This was the highest winning score since 1919, when Walter Hagen won with the same total at Brae Burn. Bobby's rounds, 76-77-79-77, added up 309, and he finished in a tie for eleventh place, along with Bobby Cruickshank, Leo Diegel, and Eddie Loos.

The first two rounds certainly look bad enough; yet nobody was scoring well, and when Bobby stood on the thirteenth tee of the third round he was in what might be called a winning position. Harry Cooper was leading at the time, and Bobby was just one stroke behind him. And Bobby was going well, at last. It appeared that a 70 or a 71 was the worst he should do.

And right there, as he said later, the tournament blew up in his face.

The thirteenth was a pitch-hole of 160 yards. Bobby pulled his mashie-shot into a ditch, far to the left; hacked the ball out of the ditch into a bunker; took two to get out; and finished with a 6 on a par-3 hole. The jolt was sufficient to upset the narrowly balanced equilibrium of the game he had just found. At the long fifteenth, a hole he played wretchedly all through the tournament, he took another 6. He finished with a 79, as high a score as he ever returned in the national open.

The 77 in the afternoon completed Bobby's poorest showing of the eleven United States opens in which he played. And it accounted for a sudden decision to sail for Britain, to have a try at the British open. My first news of this decision was received in a manner which perhaps excuses recounting.

I left Oakmont without waiting to see the play-off of the tie between Armour and Cooper, because the play-off was to be on June 17 and I had an engagement to be married in New York on June 18. Mrs. Keeler and I then planned to sail on the *Aquitania*, just after midnight between the days of June 20 and 21. The afternoon before sailing I called at the offices of the United States Golf Association to see the secretary, Tommy McMahon.

"Here's a telegram you may be interested in," he said, as soon as he saw me.

The telegram was from Bobby. He inquired if the entries for the British open were closed. If not, would Mr. McMahon cable his entry?

"It's cabled," said Tommy.

And the following Saturday, Bobby sailed on the *Transylvania*, accompanied by his father and two Atlanta friends, Charlie Freeman and Sherwood Hurt, landing at Glasgow with five days left for practice at St. Andrews before the qualifying rounds of the British open.

So I saw Bobby in that championship, too.

It was quite a competition, at any rate from an American point of view. Bobby played badly in practice; went over to Gleneagles the day before the qualifying rounds and seemed to get the touch; lost it again in the first qualifying round; and then, playing on the New Course, did a 71 for the second, which tied the record, and, naturally, put him in the championship easily enough.

"This championship," writes Mr. Bernard Darwin, "will always be remembered for the fact that Bobby performed the wholly indecent and profane feat of holing four rounds of the links in a score of three under an average of 4's."

And the total score of this whimsically expressed admiration, 285, thus far is the lowest registered in a British open championship, and a stroke lower than the American record by Chick Evans, in 1916.

And Bobby's first round, of 68, was the first time he had broken 70 in a major open championship.

I shall always feel that a bad second hole started him off on that amazing spin. After an uneventful par 4 at the first, a long drive from the second tee rolled into Cheape's bunker, and the ball was tucked up close to the steep front wall. Bobby failed to get out with the first blast; the second was barely in the fairway; his pitch was 30 feet from the flag—and he rammed down the putt for a 5 which had looked terribly like a 6.

Two more holes in par 4 followed, and then he broke away.

The fifth hole—the Hole o' Cross it is called, because it shares a vast green with the thirteenth—is a big one, of 533 yards. Bobby followed a great drive with a spoon shot that just made the front edge of the putting surface. The ball was 120 feet from the flag. As he walked toward it he said in a low tone to the marker:

"That's the longest putt I ever saw!"

And he holed it, for an eagle 3.

That was the start. From there in he did not miss a putt of under a dozen feet. He holed a 30-footer for a 2 at the eighth—one of the only two short holes on the Old Course at St. Andrews. He holed a 20-footer for a par 4, after missing his second shot at the thirteenth. He played the first nine holes in 32 and the last nine in 36, and he used 29 putts in the round. The first thing he said to me about it, after he had escaped into the clubhouse from a genial mob of autograph-seekers, was:

"Did you ever see as absolutely crazy a round of golf?"

In some ways, the answer is no. Because it is a very famous round I append the card, with par of the Old Course:

```
Par (out) ...... 444  454  434—36
Jones .......... 454  433  423—32

Par (in) ....... 434  454  454—37—73
Jones .......... 434  454  444—36—68
```

This set Bobby well in front, right at the start. It was the only national open championship of his career in which he led all the way, and I know that he found making the pace a fearful strain that increased with every round. His second card was 72. His third was 73—the worst score he turned in; exactly par. He went into the final round with a lead of four strokes, and he started badly—through the Hole o' Cross his score read 4-5-5-4-5. Three over 4's. His lead seemed to be going. I had set out with him, thinking only to see him well started and then turn back to see how his pursuers were faring. And now I couldn't leave him. Neither, it seemed, could some thirty thousand others—the biggest gallery I had ever seen.

Bobby's face was set and sunken and he never

changed his expression as he picked up a stroke with a birdie 3 at the 370-yard sixth. He picked up another 3 at the 303-yard ninth and was out in 37—not too bad. But that 20-foot putt at the ninth had started the fireworks. He drove the tenth green, 312 yards, for another birdie 3. At the short and dangerous eleventh he nearly holed a 2 from the back of the green. At the twelfth, 314 yards, he ran a short approach up two feet from the stick. That made four 3's in a row. From the fifth through the twelfth, he had changed his card from three above 4's to two below. The championship was in the bag. He finished with a 72, nearly holing a long putt from the Valley of Sin at the front of the last green.

As to the scene immediately following that round, I shall quote Mr. Darwin's *Green Memories* once more:

The scene that followed his last putt was wonderful. Not even when Francis Ouimet beat Vardon and Ray was there such a riot of joy. Personally I thought that Bobby was going to be killed in the very hour of victory. "One moment stood he as the angels stand," shaking hands with Andrew Kirkaldy, and "the next he was not," for the crowd, unmindful of anything or anybody else, stormed up the slope and swallowed him. It was a real relief when, after what seemed whole minutes, Bobby reappeared, his putter held high over his head, borne aloft on admiring shoulders. It was a wonderful demonstration of personal popularity, but it was something more than that. It showed that the Scottish crowd, the most passionately patriotic crowd in the world, knows a great golfer when it sees one, and knew that Bobby was by so far the greatest there that it could not bear anyone else to win.

Fred Robson and Aubrey Boomer, English professionals, tied for second place at 291, six strokes behind the new record, and also tied with the former record, held jointly by James Braid at Prestwick and Bobby at St. Anne's.

When the cup was awarded to him for the second time in two years, Bobby, in a graceful little speech, brought out the fact that he was a member of the Royal and Ancient Golf Club of St. Andrews.

"And I'm not going to carry the cup back home with me," he said. "I'm going to ask the Royal and Ancient Golf Club to keep it for the year of my championship."

You may imagine whether that Scottish crowd cheered then!

So Bobby went home without the cup, after all, but very happy. He felt that he had atoned for the Oakmont bust, and he went out to Minneapolis, where the national amateur was to be played at the Minikahda Club the week of August 22, in a cheerful frame of mind, but playing terrible golf once more.

As at Inwood, he seemed unable to break 80 in practice without a struggle. And as at Inwood he came on his game gradually, and when he needed it most. Only he did not, as at Inwood, imperil his chances by a slump toward the finish.

Bobby did a 75 in the first qualifying round at Minikahda, and I know he was badly worried. He was several strokes back of a couple of brilliant youngsters—Phil Finlay and Gene Homans —and that circumstance didn't bother him, but he was wondering if he should get better next day, or get worse and fail to qualify. At last he decided that the thing to do was not merely to try to qualify; he would go out there in the second round to win the medal, if he could—to shoot the works.

The short third hole had been annoying him; a simple pitch of 141 yards. He had been missing his par on it consistently, and he was worried when, after two easy holes in par, he reached it in this round. Sure enough, his pitch was short. And then he holed a chip-shot for a 2.

The break had come. When he reached the turn, he had a card of 31. He came home in 36, and was medalist with 75-67—142, in a tie for the record and three strokes ahead of Harrison Johnston, who had beaten out Homans and Finlay.

In the ensuing match-play Bobby had one close call—and it was a terribly close one. His first opponent was Maurice McCarthy. The big Irishman was not playing especially well, but Bobby's game again had gone sour on him and through the twelfth hole he was 1 down. At the 547-yard thirteenth he looked certain to be 2 down. McCarthy was well on with his third and Bobby's pitch was hooked to the long grass at the left of the green, and his chip was a dozen feet short. McCarthy's first putt was dead for a par 5, and Bobby had a side hill putt of the rainbow variety to save a half. I could hardly watch that putt. I felt, deep down inside, that if it didn't drop, Bobby's goose was cooked.

He putted, at least a yard out of line, up the slope.

It dropped.

He still was 1 down, but now he managed to stick exactly to par and McCarthy needed a 5 at each of the last three holes, and Bobby won the match, 2 up.

He got by the second 18-hole match that afternoon, beating Homans 3-2, and then he went through the 36-hole engagements in his most convincing style. He defeated Harrison Johnston 10-9, Francis Ouimet 11-10, and then, in the finals, he met Chick Evans for the third and last time. Chick had beaten him in the western amateur at Memphis in 1920; Bobby had won in the national amateur at Baltusrol in 1926; and this was a sort of rubber.

Bobby was "hot" and the cards for the first nine tell the story of the match:

```
Par (out) ...... 443  543  435—35
Jones .......... 433  443  433—31
Evans .......... 444  543  446—38
```

The eagle 3 at the ninth probably was the most-talked-of shot in the Minikahda tournament. This hole is 512 yards, a dog-leg, with the finish up a steep slope to a small, hilltop green. Bobby, working his hardest against his traditional rival, put his back into a huge drive which opened up the green for the second shot—but that second shot, if he would reach the green, was something like 230 yards, all uphill. Bobby laid into the ball with a spoon from a rather tight lie. The shot carried to the front of the green, as if pitched from a mashie. It rolled straight for the flag.

It stopped twenty inches short, after more than a furlong in the air.

Bobby never seemed to think much of this shot, which, he insisted, was a perfectly simple one to play. But I am in agreement with some ten thousand other persons, that it was one of the finest wood shots in the record of major championships.

Chick was 5 down at the turn. He lost the tenth to a birdie 3, and won the eleventh with a 2. Bobby had a string of seven 3's in the first eleven holes of the match, which ended, 8-7, at the eleventh hole of the afternoon round.

And though I never mentioned it to Bobby, or he to me, this 1927 amateur championship at Minikahda went in the book as one more consecutive year in which Bobby Jones was a champion of the United States, in the string he was trying to stretch to six.

Minikahda made it five in a row.

CHAPTER XVIII

A PUTT AT WINGED FOOT

IT IS to be hoped that the uninterrupted rush of incident and action in this narrative will not engender in the reader's mind the idea that Bobby Jones did little or nothing except play golf; that impression would be greatly in error. His tournament season, which he observed so closely in these later years, really was a brief affair. In the last eight years of his competitive career, including three ventures to Britain, Bobby averaged just three months of each twelve for the period which comprised his play in the major championships and his journeyings to and from them. And except for the three years in which he went to Great Britain, most of the tournament season was spent quietly at home, with no more time at golf than is devoted regularly by some stodgy banker who likes an afternoon round with his habitual foursome whenever it is convenient.

Bobby without any doubt played less formal or competitive golf in the eight years of his championships than any other first-rank amateur or professional golfer in the world. I remember a winter season, preceding one of his most successful tournament periods, in which for six months he played exactly ten rounds, and not one formal match. Early in 1928 he finished his law studies at Emory University, Atlanta, and assumed a desk as junior member of the law firm of Jones, Evins, Powers, and Jones, being about the same time admitted to the state and federal bars. And there was no major golf competition for him that year until the national open, June 21-24, at the Olympia Fields Country Club near Chicago.

This tournament left Bobby in the position of runner-up to Johnny Farrell after a 36-hole play-off, with a somewhat exceptional set of harrowing memories of golden opportunities tossed away.

Bobby started that tournament with a fair round of 73, which left a good many contenders ahead of him—Frank Ball, professional at Bobby's home club, East Lake, and Henry Ciuci were leading, at 70; Leonard Schmutte was 71; and Leo Diegel, Horton Smith, John Golden, and Bill Leach had 72. Of this array of first-round leaders only Leach and Ciuci finished in the first seventeen, and they were tied for sixth position. That Olympia Fields course was a puzzle for everybody.

The second day it rained, and Bobby, starting in the morning—starting times of course were reversed on the first and second days—finished without any precipitation with a good 71 and went into the lead, with 144 at the halfway mark. Walter Hagen put on the big show, that day. Playing the first nine in the afternoon without any rain, he required a bad 40. Playing the last nine in a torrential downpour, he came back in 32, and his 72 kept him very much in the chase.

Bobby carded a 73 in the third round, fighting hard all the time with an erratic drive and two jinx holes—the third and the ninth. At the latter, he never managed a par 4, and at the third he had three 6's, for no good reason except a drive that seemed always a bit off line.

Still, this left him two strokes ahead of the field, with a score of 217. Ciuci was next, with 219; Hagen had 220; Farrell and George Von Elm, 222; and Roland Hancock, 223. Ciuci with a wild 80 faded out of the picture in the fourth round; the rest of them had a grim sort of mêlée.

Bobby started his last round, as usual, with a birdie 4. He clicked away steadily to the fifth hole, and there picked up another birdie. And there, so far as human reckoning applied, he seemed to have the open championship in the bag. The jinx hole —the third—was behind him. He was past the toughest part of the course two strokes under par. He had a lead which he knew was at least five or six strokes on the field.

And this is what happened. It is a sort of confession.

Bobby was worn out, fighting the course. His erratic driving—that course at Olympia Fields is essentially one which requires accurate placing of tee-shots—had kept him in trouble much of the time. He was tired of struggling. And he had a big lead, after all. I think, after that fifth hole of the final round at Olympia Fields, that Bobby looked more like a certain winner than he looked at the same stage of any other open championship, even at St. Andrews the year before.

It seemed in the bag. And Bobby, weary and worn, made the fatal mistake of telling himself that he would just coast in from there.

Par beginning with the sixth hole is 3-4-3-4-4 for the next five holes.

Bobby's card for these holes showed 5-6-4-5-5. Seven strokes lost to par, in five successive holes. That is what coasting can do, even to Bobby Jones, in an open championship.

The jolt came at the short sixth, where he took a No. 4 iron and played a soft shot instead of hitting decisively with a mashie. His left elbow relaxed a shade too soon—he quit on the stroke. The ball was pulled to a ditch from which he did well to get a 5. The rest of the *débâcle* came naturally, trying to steer the shots. He had coasted out of a great lead.

After a sad 5 at the tenth, failing to get home with an iron second, the strain pulled him together, and he finished the spin in par—but the card was a 77. His total was 294. Hagen and Macfarlane with bad fourth rounds passed up the chance he gave them, but Johnny Farrell with a fine 72 picked up five strokes and went into a tie. Roland Hancock, a young professional from Wilmington, N. C., had them both beaten as he stood on the seventeenth tee of the last round after a wonderful burst of golf. Par 4-5 at the last two holes would have given him the championship, with a round of 69 and two strokes to spare. But the strain and, it must be said, a wildly enthusiastic gallery, wrecked him. He finished 6-6, where 5-5 would have won. He was third, with 295. Hagen and Von Elm were tied in fourth place, at 296.

The play-off next day between Bobby and Johnny Farrell was the first one in the history of the United States Golf Association at 36 holes. Bobby started with a birdie at 4 at the first hole and picked up a stroke. Thereafter he was never in the lead until the thirtieth. Bobby was three behind at the end of the morning round, 73 to 70. He started with another birdie in the afternoon and with 4-4 collared Johnny, who started 6-5. Then his second 6 of the play-off at the jinx hole —the third—put him two behind again. Once more he squared, and then lost two more strokes with another 6 at his other jinx hole, the ninth. Johnny started home 5-5-5, Bobby started 4-4-4, and was in front for the first time since the first hole. It was raining, but the gallery didn't seem to know it. Farrell squared with his third 2 of the play-off at the short thirteenth, and Bobby went down for the last time at the sixteenth, when his pitch nearly hit the flag and trickled off into the rough.

Par at the last two holes was 4-5 and it afforded one of the greatest finishes in golfing annals. Johnny, leading by a stroke, planted his pitch five feet from the flag, while Bobby was thirty feet away. In the pinch, Bobby holed his birdie 3, and Johnny matched it. At the last hole it looked as if Bobby might square, when his second shot was just off the green in a smooth hollow while Johnny's was in the rough, sixty yards away. Johnny pitched on, ten feet from the stick, and Bobby chipped dead for a birdie 4. . . . Then Johnny holed his putt, for the championship.

Thus far in history, that is the greatest playoff in any open championship, each competitor finishing with two holes under par, and a single stroke difference. Farrell scored 70-73—143. Bobby scored 73-71—144, the same as in his first two rounds of the competition. Also, it was level 4's. But this time it was not good enough.

And so Bobby's first chance in 1928 to extend his string of national championships slipped away on a beautiful ten-foot putt of Johnny Farrell's, and he went home to Atlanta to do some work and, six weeks later, to start getting in shape for the Walker Cup international match at the Chicago Golf Club, August 30 and 31. It was Great Britain's time to send a team to this country, and Bobby had been named captain of the American side, and the Americans had never lost a match in the four that had been played, and Bobby felt his responsibility heavily.

His practice rounds were at the Biltmore Forest Country Club, Asheville, the Old Elm Club, Chicago, the Flossmoor Country Club, and the Chicago Golf Club, and I believe that his play on these courses was the finest stretch of scoring over any similar period for his entire career. I kept his cards.

On four different courses, none easy, the cards were 69-71-69-68-68-68-67-68-67-70. This is an average of 68.5. It is 35 strokes under 4's, in ten rounds.

The round at the Flossmoor Country Club, where Bobby was beaten in the second round of the 1923 amateur championship, was a funny one, and prodigiously spectacular. Members of both the British and American Walker Cup teams were invited to play in a one-round medal competition for the Warren K. Wood memorial trophy. Bobby played in the last foursome of the day. Johnny Dawson had finished early with a 71, and it looked like the winning score. Par for the course, of nearly 7,000 yards, is 72—a tough card. Bobby started rather loosely and pitched into the lake at the short seventh hole, at which stage he was three over 4's.

I think that 5 at the tiny seventh hole annoyed Bobby and he began to bear down. At any rate, starting with the eighth hole, a par 4, he reeled off the longest string of 3's he ever put together on any course or in any event.

Following is the card of the Flossmoor course, with that odd score he brought in, to win the Warren K. Wood memorial bowl:

```
Par (out) ...... 535  444  344—36
Jones .......... 445  445  533—37

Par (in) ....... 534  344  445—36—72
Jones .......... 333  334  344—30—67
```

The string of 3's ran along to seven, with a startling eagle at the long tenth hole, where, from a bunker by the green, he chipped out for another 3. Beginning with the eighth hole, he did nine consecutive holes in 28 strokes, par for them being 35. He had 28 putts in the round. If the 30-footer at the last hole had dropped, he'd have realized a pet ambition—to break 30 on either side of a regular golf course. He did a 28 on nine consecutive holes, in this round. But that was along in the middle; not on either side.

In the international match at the Chicago Golf Club, the Americans won by the widest margin yet recorded—11 points to 1. Bobby, the captain, defeated Phil Perkins, British amateur champion, 13-12, and he and Chick Evans in the foursomes defeated Major Hezlet and W. L. Hope, 5-3. And then all hands moved along to Boston, where the national amateur was played at the Brae Burn Country Club, September 10-15.

As in the 1927 championship, this tournament, for Bobby, turned on one match—the 18-hole bout in the second round with Ray Gorton, a Brae Burn member, and holder of the course record.

Bobby was over the peak again when he reached Brae Burn. That long string of sub-par rounds, a dozen in all, through the international match, seemed to be all the golf he had for the time being. His first qualifying round was 77; his second 74. He qualified merely comfortably. George Voigt, with 71 and 72, was the medalist, at 143. The top score was 157, and Bobby, with 151, was in fifth place.

Bobby got by his first 18-hole match, with J. W. Brown, winning 4-3. Then came what turned out to be the crucial match of the championship.

Against Gorton, Bobby went incredibly off his game to the turn, taking 42 strokes for the first nine holes—and still he was square, for Gorton was as wild as he. Then came the fireworks.

The tenth hole was 491 yards in length. Gorton smacked a brassie second twelve feet past the flag and sank the putt for an eagle, while Bobby was getting a very fine birdie 4. He was 1 down.

The eleventh hole is of 463 yards, rated a par 4 on the card. Gorton was straight with his drive and his second was on the green, twenty feet from the flag. Bobby's drive was a long one, sliced to the deep rough, with a small tree nearly in his line and a clump of tall trees directly between the ball and the green, which was 200 yards away.

The trees made it necessary for him to get elevation on the shot promptly; the deep grass constituted a lie from which most expert players would have used a niblick or a spade; and the hole seemed hopelessly lost, which would have put him 2 down. Bobby took a No. 4 iron, swung as hard as he could, tearing up a great strip of turf and long grass, and the fascinated gallery saw the ball soar over the trees and descend on the green, five yards from the hole.

This shot, Bobby says himself, probably was the best iron he ever played in competition.

After which, apparently not in the least perturbed, Gorton holed his 20-footer for a birdie 3, and Bobby his 15-footer for the half.

Still 1 down, Bobby squared at the short

twelfth, and went down again when Gorton holed a ten-footer for a birdie 4 at the long thirteenth. They halved the still longer fourteenth with par 5, and Bobby squared at the fifteenth, where Gorton was bunkered. They halved the sixteenth and then came a terribly tricky hole of 255 yards, a par 3, with a drive from a hilltop tee to a rather small green in a sort of valley.

Neither hit the green from the tee and Bobby was bunkered. Gorton chipped close for his 3, and Bobby's blast from the sand left him a putt of seven feet on the most deceptive green on the course. . . . Watching from the hillside above, I thought the ball would never get as far as the hole, it went so slowly over the glassy surface. When it dropped out of sight, I most surprisingly found myself sitting on the grass. I had dropped, too.

The eighteenth at Brae Burn required a tremendous carry from the tee, 220 yards over a mound and a brook, straight across the fairway. Bobby was far over, but sliced to a place behind a similar cross-bank, farther on. Gorton popped his drive high in the air, into the thick woods at the left. He played out at right-angles and his third shot, a long brassie, was still a hundred yards short of the green. Bobby seemed certain to win, when his own third was twenty feet past the flag, while Gorton's pitch, his fourth shot, was five yards past. Bobby rolled the putt up dead for a 5 and almost in Gorton's line. Then Gorton sank the putt, for a half.

Gorton collapsed in earnest at the first extra hole. Bobby's drive was in the middle and Gorton's was in the woods at the right, this time back of a wood-pile. He played out sideways again and his third was at the back of the green, while Bobby's second was four yards from the flag. At that, I nearly had heart-failure once more in that match. Gorton's long putt hit the cup for a par 4. But the ball stayed out.

That was the tournament. Next day, beginning the 36-hole bouts, Bobby beat John Beck of England 14-13. Then he beat Phil Finlay 13-12, and, in the finals, Phil Perkins, British champion, 10-9. Former champions went by the board at a great rate in the 18-hole matches. George Von Elm, Jess Sweetser, Max Marston, and Francis Ouimet, all were out the first day, at Brae Burn.

And at the close of 1928 Bobby had been national champion six years in a row. The ambition of 1925 had been realized. And yet neither of us said anything about it. I think perhaps we both, by that time, had the hope that the string might be longer, and we were afraid of saying so—it might break the charm.

The charm carried on past Winged Foot, in the national open of 1929. But there it had to be good for a twelve-foot putt at the seventy-second green; a twelve-foot, curving putt, for a tie with Al Espinosa; a twelve-foot putt that was the most important stroke of Bobby Jones's career.

Working around to that stroke through three days of play, Bobby had brought in his first card under 70 in the American open; had been in the lead, and out of it, and in it again, and finally was tied. He had started his first round with a calamitous 6 at the long par-4 first hole, and a bad 5 at the 225-yard third. Then he had regained two of the lost strokes at the 514-yard fifth hole, with a great drive, a spoon, and a 40-foot putt for an eagle 3, and, as in his first round in 1927 at St. Andrews, that started him off on a spectacular spin. He reached the turn in 38, still two strokes above the card, but started home 3-3-3-3-3, one of them an eagle, at the 500-yard twelfth. Finishing smoothly in 4's, he had done the last nine in 31, and with a card of 69 he was leading the field at the end of the first day. Al Espinosa was next, with 70, and Gene Sarazen third with 71.

This latter pair played early in the second day,

before the hard rain which began soon after noon, and at the halfway mark they were tied for the lead, at 142. Bobby caught the rain and his 75 pulled him back to 144, in a tie with Densmore Shute. George Von Elm and Tommy Armour brought in the two finest rounds of the tournament, 70 and 71, playing all the way in a torrential downpour; Armour at this stage was 145 and Von Elm 149.

The rain slowed up the big course for the finishing two rounds on Saturday, and Bobby, playing with great confidence and boldness, holed the third round in a beautiful 71 and once more was out in front. His nearest pursuers, Sarazen and Espinosa, had required 76 and 77, and the third-round totals were: Jones, 215; Sarazen, 218; Espinosa, 219; Shute, 220; Armour, 221; and Von Elm, 223.

Sarazen and Espinosa started ahead of Bobby in the last round and by the time he had played the seventh hole, just missing a birdie 2, his position seemed as secure as anything can be, in so uncertain a game as golf. He had par 4-5 left for a 36 on that side. Espinosa had done a 36 for the nine but had run into a dreadful 8 at the long twelfth hole. Sarazen had taken 41 strokes for the first nine, and seemed likewise out of the picture.

Then, after one tiny mistake, Bobby took a ghastly 7 at the eighth hole. He followed a bold and powerful drive by holding up a long pitch just a shade too much against a right-hand wind, the ball bounded into a deep bunker; his recovery sent it trickling across the green into another bunker; he blasted from that clear over into the original trap; barely got out with his fifth stroke, and took two putts.

Now it had become a driving finish once more, and under the strain he picked up a birdie 4 at the ninth and was out in 38, still with what looked like a commanding lead. But the experience in the bunkers had shaken him terribly; he felt that he must not get in any more of them; and he fired an iron clear over the well-trapped tenth green and needed a hard 4 against a par of 3. Still, he got past the long twelfth with a clear lead at that point of six strokes over Espinosa.

Now, here is a remarkable illustration of the curious psychological effect of strain in an open golf championship. Espinosa, struggling desperately until that terrible 8 at the twelfth hole, walked off that green with the conviction that it was all over—that he didn't have a chance. The strain was gone. And he finished the last six holes with an incredibly brilliant run of four 4's and two 3's, for a round of 75, and a total of 294.

Behind him, Bobby was still struggling. He lost a stroke at the 230-yard thirteenth; got his par 4 at the fourteenth; and then, following a sliced drive back of a clump of trees, pitched out to a hanging lie, fired his third over the green into very deep rough, failed to get out of the hay with his fourth—and another 7 went on his card. He had now lost most of his lead over Espinosa, who had finished. Bobby, with three holes to play, needed 4-4-4 to go ahead, by a single stroke, and the sixteenth was a par 5. The wind was behind him. A big drive and a strong iron put the ball on the green, twenty feet from the flag—and then he was five feet short with his first putt, and missed the next one. His margin was wiped out. He had to finish 4-4, to tie.

He got the first 4 properly enough. Then, with all the gallery on the course collected about him and around the home green, he followed a good drive with a pulled pitch, and the ball rolled down the slope of a deep bunker at the left of the green, stopping in the grass before it reached the sand.

And his chip was bad. The ball lay twelve feet from the hole. And it was that—or nothing.

Or worse than nothing. If Bobby missed that putt, he would have gone as high as 80 for the first time in his ten American open championships. He would have finished second to Espinosa—and that of itself was all right. But in finishing second, he would have chucked away a lead of six strokes, and one more, in the last six holes of an open championship. And that, as I knew in a sort of bewildering flash, would be held by Bobby as an eternal disgrace; a blot on his record never to be wiped out.

Everybody in that huge gallery knew exactly what the situation was, when Bobby came up out of the deep bunker and walked toward the ball. Al Watrous, his playing companion as in the last two rounds of the British open at St. Anne's, crouched on the green. Tack Ramsay, holding the flag, took it from the cup and knelt on one knee, not to obstruct the gallery vision. Bobby stood up to putt in a queer, breathing silence that was pressing into my ears; but it seemed that somewhere, very far off, I could hear a bell ringing slowly.

A movement of the gallery had shut off my view, but I couldn't have looked, anyway. And I could tell with a deadly certainty what was happening. . . . The breathing ceased. He was addressing the ball. . . . A thin click, and the beginning of a kind of sigh—the ball was on its way. The sigh grew louder . . . it changed to a gasp. . . . Missed!

No!

The gasp changed to a roar, the stunning crash of a thunderbolt that strikes at your feet.

The ball had rolled, slowly and more slowly, to the rim of the hole; hesitated—stopped. And then . . .

Well, then it had dropped.

CHAPTER XIX

IT WAS Al Watrous, a few minutes later in the locker-room of the Winged Foot Club, who described that putt to me. It was twelve feet, said Al, and the slope of the green made it necessary to "borrow" about ten inches from the left of the straight line. Al said that the distance was so nicely gauged that had the hole been a circle, four and a quarter inches in diameter, on the green, the ball would have stopped right in the middle of it. He added that it was the finest putt he ever saw, whether anything depended on it or not.

And everything had depended on this one.

Bobby, apparently inspired by his narrow escape, played his best golf of the week next day, after starting with another bad 6 at the first hole. He finished the play-off with cards of 72-69—141, winning rather easily from Espinosa, who was weary and stale.

And a couple of months later, the first week in September, Bobby was in the 1929 national amateur championship on the beautiful Pebble Beach course at Del Monte, California, with what looked to be a very fine chance at three records. He might win his fifth amateur title, breaking the tie with Jerry Travers. He might make it three amateur championships in a row, which hadn't been done. And he might equal Chick Evans's record of 1916, winning the open and the amateur the same season.

Instead of all which, he made another record, for himself.

He lost in the first round.

The critics were kind enough with explanations. They called attention to the exceptionally fine golf Bobby had played in exhibition matches at Los Angeles and practice rounds at Del Monte —and every round he played was an exhibition match, in California, where everybody was almost absurdly curious and determined to see him. As a matter of fact, I think he never played better before any championship than he did in California, and it is quite possible that he had lost a measure of the essential keenness by the time he had worked through the qualifying rounds to a tie at 145 with Eugene Homans for the low medal.

Be that as it may, Bobby was paired with Johnny Goodman of Omaha in the first match. And he started 5-6-4, losing the first three holes, two by his own bad play and the third to a good putt for a birdie 3 by Goodman. Then he settled down and after the short twelfth the match was square. A lapse at the thirteenth, where his second followed Goodman's into a bunker, kept him to a half at that hole—he hopped a stymie, indeed, to get it. Then, on the long fourteenth, with his own ball nearly as far in two strokes as Goodman's in three, Bobby tried to cut a short pitch too finely; the ball caught the top rim of a deep bunker, and in place of the birdie 4 he was after he lost the hole with a 6, Goodman holing a six-foot putt. Goodman finished the round in par precisely, with a great spoon shot to the perilous 220-yard seventeenth, and Bobby could not pick up a hole, losing 1 down.

The enormous gallery appeared heart-broken. It seemed to have had a childlike faith that the open champion would be on display all week. Harrison Johnston, after a close call in a 39-hole battle with George Voigt, went on to defeat Dr. O. F. Willing in the finals.

Bobby was not particularly depressed by his first-round exit. After all, he had won the open.

And 1929 was the seventh consecutive year of championship. There was quite a lot of comfort in that.

The year 1930 offered what might be termed a substantial program in golf, for Bobby. He was captain again of the American Walker Cup team for the biennial match, to be played this time at Sandwich, England; and this meant he would play in the British amateur, which followed the Walker match, and the British open. Of course he intended to play also in the American open and the American amateur; it would be the third time in his career he had competed in all four major championships in the same season, in an attack on what George Trevor called the Impregnable Quadrilateral of Golf.

Whether Bobby had any idea, at the beginning of the 1930 season, that it was to be his last in competitive golf, I do not know. I do know that the recurrent strain of major competition was increasingly unwelcome. His uninterrupted succession of national championships, with the various British successes, had established him as the leading golfer of the world, and for years he had been ranked the favorite of every competition in which he engaged, while a considerable proportion of the sporting public seemed naïvely to expect him to win every time he started in anything connected with golf—a tribute which lost most of its force from a lack of understanding of the uncertainties of the game and the eccentricities of fortune that afflict even its best and most consistent player.

Bobby was now twenty-eight; his family included two children; he was seriously engaged in the business of law; and even two major championship tournaments a year seemed to be taking up a good deal of time and requiring a good deal of travel.

Major championships also were taking out of Bobby more than time and travel. Bobby, as Mr. Bernard Darwin said, always had played competitive golf in a manner to "take it out of himself prodigally," and, as the same writer said after seeing him finish the British open championship at Hoylake that year, it was obvious that the time was coming to call a halt.

Whether or not Bobby felt this way about it at the early beginning of the season of 1930, he prepared for the British expedition with more than usual care, and for the first time in three years he entered a winter open tournament. Indeed, he entered two of them, the Savannah open championship, and the southeastern open, at Augusta, Ga., where he might brush up his game in competition with many of the best professionals in America.

At Savannah, late in February, Horton Smith beat him out by a single stroke in an erratic and brilliant tournament in which Bobby set a new course record of 67 in the first round, Horton brought it down to 66 in the second, and Bobby placed it at 65 in the third, after which they were tied. Horton outfinished him, 71 to 72, in the fourth round, and the rest of the field was half a dozen strokes behind.

And that was the last formal competition Bobby Jones lost, to the end of his career. He won every start, of every kind, from Savannah on.

The Augusta tournament was, I believe, the best Bobby ever played. Two courses were used, the Hill Course of the Augusta Country Club, and the Forrest Hills-Ricker hotel course, with a good, stiff par of 72 and 71, respectively. Starting on the Hill Course, Bobby's four rounds were 72-72-69-71—284, including a careless lapse at the last three holes of the last round, when he was eighteen strokes ahead of the field. He finished two strokes better than par for the tournament, and thirteen strokes ahead of Horton Smith, who was second.

It was while Bobby was playing his fourth round that Bobby Cruickshank, who had finished earlier, asked me if I knew what was going to happen in the coming season. I said I'd like to know.

"Well," he said, "Bobby is just too good. He's going to Britain, and he's going to win the British amateur and the British open, and then he's coming back here and win the national open and the national amateur. They'll never stop him, this year."

I didn't tell Bobby this. As for believing it myself—I couldn't even regard it seriously. This was the Impregnable Quadrilateral that Bobby Cruickshank was talking about. No man ever had taken more than half of it in any one season before.

We sailed on the *Mauretania* late in April, with the American Walker Cup team, and Mary went with Bobby this time, and quite a party of Atlanta people. Bobby was comfortable over the state of his game, since the Augusta tournament; his iron play, and especially his pitching, had been more accurate than in years, with a lovely little right-to-left "draw" in the shots that meant power and crispness and a deadly line.

And somewhere on the voyage Bobby lost the

knack, or most of it. He ascertained afterward—
after the British campaign, indeed—what the
trouble was; a simple little variation of stance, so
that the ball was a bit too far back toward the
line of the right heel; a tiny thing, but it was as
near as possible to costing him two British championships.

So Bobby in his preliminary practice before
the international match at Sandwich, and in the
match itself, was struggling with the irons and
the pitching tools. But he played well enough to
defeat Roger Wethered, 9-8, in the singles, and,
with Dr. Willing, to win their section of the
foursomes, 8-7, from Rex Hartley and T. A.
Torrance. The American team again won easily,
10 points to 2, and the Prince of Wales came
down to Sandwich by plane both days to watch
the match—he and Bobby had been partners in
a foursome a few days before, at Sunningdale,
against Sir Philip Sassoon and Harrison Johnston, American amateur champion; and a very
good battle ended all square.

Then old St. Andrews again, and the British
amateur championship, with 270 entries and eight
rounds of match-play for the winner to get by, all
but the final match over the sudden-death route
of 18 holes.

Bobby had four desperate encounters on his way to the last round, and the first of them came at the very start, with a chap named Syd Roper of Nottinghamshire. Bobby never had heard of Mr. Roper, and naturally he made inquiries about him. He was told that Roper was a "fair sort" of golfer who would shoot a lot of 5's at him. According to my count, when that match finally ended, Mr. Roper had discharged just fifteen 4's and one 5. He was beaten 3-2. But that round would have stopped anybody else in the tournament that day, except Bobby. And Bobby had the extraordinary luck of a freak start, which put him three holes in the lead, in the first four holes—which Roper did precisely in par.

This was 4-4-4-4. And Bobby started 3-4-3-2. And the long fifth hole, a par 5, was halved with a birdie 4 by each player.

The deuce at the fourth hole came from the most-talked-of shot of the championship.

The hole is of 427 yards and at the end of a long drive down the wind Bobby's ball rolled into the Cottage bunker, nearly 300 yards from the tee. The ball lay cleanly on the sand, in a position in which an expert can apply a controlling backspin as definitely as from a lie on good turf.

Bobby played the shot with a mashie-niblick, a tall, rather steep pitch.

I was standing directly behind the large green when the feather of white sand came spurting up from the bunker, 140 yards away. The ball descended lightly, just beyond a little rise at the front of the green; the spin took hold promptly, and instead of bounding the ball rolled and seemed to slide over the glassy surface, slower and slower, and at last trickled into the hole without touching the flagstaff.

"I have traveled eight thousand miles to see this tournament," I heard one man in the gallery say, "and that shot is worth it all, and twice over!"

Roper in place of folding up played with a vast steadiness and determination. He came back with a birdie 4 at the long fifth, and Bobby had to work his hardest to end the match at the sixteenth, 3-2.

Three more hard matches came on successive days, leading into the final round with Wethered. These were with Cyril Tolley, British amateur champion; Harrison Johnston, American amateur champion; and George Voigt, one of the very toughest of the American entries—it may be seen that Bobby's path to the finals lacked something of being one of primroses.

Tolley, one of the most formidable of adversaries when in the humor, was in the humor for that bout. Five times Bobby got him down; five times the big Englishman squared; they never were more than a hole apart; and going to the seventeenth, the famous Road Hole, they were level.

Their drives were about alike, with Tolley a bit ahead. Bobby played a big iron to pass a small, deep pot-bunker at the edge of the green and send the ball to the side next to the eighteenth tee. He had a break, there. The shot was struck a shade too emphatically, the ball came up on the first bound and struck in the gallery back of the green, stopping nearly where he had designed. Tolley's iron was short and the ball was exactly back of the little bunker and well below the putting surface. The green was very narrow at that point; it sloped away from the shot, and it appeared there was no possible way to stop the ball near the flag. Bobby seemed to ease up a bit here; his long approach putt was badly calculated, and the ball slid away on the slope of the green, coming to rest a good eight feet from the hole.

And then Tolley, with a niblick, executed the most exquisite little pitch imaginable, dropping the ball just at the crest of the bunker, so that it trickled down close to the pin—dead for a birdie 4.

The tables were turned. Again it was a putt for his life. And Bobby sank it, for the half. They halved the next hole—the eighteenth. Bobby won the first extra hole, with a par 4, playing steadily while Tolley missed the green with his pitch and failed to get close with a chip, so that Bobby's first putt partly stymied him.

Next day Bobby seemed to have the American champion well in hand at the thirteenth, where Johnston was 4 down with five to play. But Johnston had other ideas. He won the long fourteenth with a birdie 4; won the fifteenth when Bobby pulled his second shot to a bunker; halved the sixteenth by holing a 12-foot putt; and won the Road Hole, the seventeenth, with a great birdie 4 against a par 5.

The strain was telling on both players, and their second shots to the home hole were away up at one corner of the big green. Johnston rolled an approach putt close for a par 4 and Bobby left himself a tough one, of seven feet. He managed to hole it, for a half, and the match, 1 up.

In the match with Voigt, Bobby was down near the finish for the only time in the championship. He evidently was feeling the strain of the long competition and the numerous battles, and George was outplaying him, being 2 up with five to play. Bobby then managed to hold on while George sliced his drive just enough at the long fourteenth so that the cross-wind carried it out of bounds, and then, at the sixteenth, hit his drive plump into a little bunker called the Principal's Nose. This squared the count, but George outplayed him on the seventeenth, so that Bobby was left with yet another desperate sort of putt for a half in a birdie 4—it was of twelve feet, identical in length with the famous last putt at Winged Foot.

Bobby said an odd thing about that putt, a few minutes after the match, which he won at the last green, 1 up.

"When I stood up to it," he told me, "I had a feeling I'd never had before. I felt that all through this tournament something had been taking care of me, and that however I struck that putt, it was going down."

Well, it went down. But it must be said that he struck it with a very beautiful precision, for all the strain and the terrible importance of that stroke.

The pressure, for Bobby, was somewhat re-relieved by getting into a 36-hole match at last, in the final round with Roger Wethered, and after the tall Englishman had held him level the first nine holes he went away steadily to win, 7-6, at the twelfth green of the afternoon round, from which a stalwart police escort convoyed him nearly a mile to the clubhouse through a milling, frantic gallery of twenty-five thousand fans.

So Bobby had won his first and only British amateur championship, in the tournament which George Duncan considers (and Bobby heartily agrees) to be the hardest golfing event in the world to win. Certainly his record in that classic is the lowest of all. He won one out of three British amateur championships in which he played. He won five out of thirteen American amateur championships. He won four out of eleven American opens. And he won three out of four British opens.

He was going into his last British open at Hoylake two weeks after the British amateur.

"Will this victory," I asked him, "inspire you with renewed enthusiasm and determination at Hoylake?"

Bobby grinned.

"Quite the contrary," he said. "I've won the British amateur—at last. My little expedition is a success, no matter what happens at Hoylake.

And I'm going to relax a bit. Mary and I are going over to Paris."

And so, while his golfing career moved on to its tremendous climax with all the seeming inevitability of a natural phenomenon, I really think Bobby enjoyed the little vacation in Paris without the slightest concern, or even thought, for the Impregnable Quadrilateral, though he had taken by brilliant escalade its steepest rampart.

At Saint-Germain, Bobby and Harrison Johnston had a fine match with André Vagliano, French amateur champion, and Marcel Dallemagne, professional title-holder, defeating them 1 up.

It is of course purely a matter of opinion, but I shall always feel that at least five other contestants were playing better golf in the British open championship of 1930 than Bobby Jones, who won it. These were the American professionals, Macdonald Smith—a transplanted Scot, Horton Smith and Leo Diegel, and the British professionals, Fred Robson and Archie Compston. Bobby has said more than once that he never worked so hard or suffered so much, in any other tournament. His driving had gone sour, and he couldn't seem to hole any of the stroke-saving long putts. On the first three holes in the first three rounds he lost five strokes to par—and they were holes which, it seemed, were ideally suited to his play. He never got away to a good start until the last round, after the giant Compston, with a marvelous 68 in the third round, had taken the lead away from him by one stroke.

And yet, when he came to the eighth hole of the last round, with all the seemingly hopeless struggling that had gone before, Bobby knew that he was well in the lead. He knew that a par 5 on that eighth hole would, in all human probability, close the door on the pursuit—and he had been doing the hole with a drive and spoon, despite its 485 yards, so a birdie 4 was not unlikely. It was the big chance to close the door.

A fine, long drive was followed by a spoon shot ending with the ball down a smooth little slope at the left-front of the green; a most plausible 4; a seemingly certain 5. As some one said later, an old lady with a croquet mallet could have saved him two strokes from that place.

He struck the little run-up too tenderly. The ball stopped on the slope. He chipped ten feet short. He went boldly for the putt. The ball slipped past, two feet. He missed, coming back. It was a 7.

The door, which should have been closed, was wide open. And two grim faces were peering through.

Sometimes I think that Bobby never did anything finer than the remainder of that round, after that smash on the button, fighting his way to a 75 and a total of 291, while behind him Leo Diegel and Macdonald Smith pressed closer and closer to the door that he should have closed and barred. At the last, in the midst of the greatest five finishing holes in the world, it came down to a blast from a bunker beside the sixteenth green, on the longest hole of the course, and the seventieth of the competition. An hour later Leo Diegel stood on that tee, and his score, after sixty-nine holes, was exactly square with Bobby's. So you may say that this hole made the difference.

The sixteenth at Hoylake is of 532 yards, at tournament stretch, the longest hole on the course; and Bobby was going after everything. A huge drive gave him the chance to get home with a spoon second, but the shot curled to the left and the ball ran into a bunker at the side of the green, lying tucked up against the front wall in such a manner that he had to stand with his right foot in the sand and his left up on the bank. It was the kind of recovery shot from which one might take—well, anything.

Bobby swung hard and up came the ball, floating in a geyser of sand, flopping on the green like a tired frog, rolling—rolling. . . . It was within four inches of holing out.

That birdie 4 made the difference. An hour later Diegel, playing the same hole, was bunkered from the tee. He took a 6. He and Bobby each finished 4-4.

Bobby's total was 291. Diegel's was 293. Macdonald Smith came in with the best card of the last round, 71, to tie with Diegel.

Bobby, as soon as he had finished his last round, went up to the secretary's room in the old clubhouse to wait for the jury to come in. I went up there to see him, several times, and as often went back down again, to see what Mac Smith and Diegel were doing. On one of these visits I asked Bobby, bluntly, when he was going to quit this sort of foolishness. That's the way it seemed, just then—a tragic sort of foolishness.

"Pretty soon, I think—and hope," said Bobby. "There's no game worth these last three days."

He told me later that when they called for him to go out on the lawn and get the cup, he hardly knew what it was all about.

I think that right there he was deciding he had had enough, no matter what happened the rest of the year.

But he sailed for home with his flag planted on two sides of the Impregnable Quadrilateral.

CHAPTER XX

O N THE boat train from London to Southampton, Cyril Tolley asked Bobby, suddenly:

"How long have you been over?"

Bobby said about six weeks.

"Well," said Cyril, "do you think you ever played quite so badly for so long a period before?"

And Bobby, going home with both major championships, said "No," before he had time to think it over. After thinking it over, he still said no. And it wasn't in the least a matter of conceit. It was the admission of fearfully hard work, and breaks that had favored him—and a vague but persistent conviction Bobby and I had shared for some years, that if you're going to win a championship, you're going to win it; and if you aren't, why, you aren't.

Bobby had won the British amateur and the

British open championships; half the Quadrilateral was captured now. But we both felt that fate had a great hand in it. And we couldn't help wondering what sort of a hand fate would play, at Interlachen—and then at Merion.

Beside the big events in Britain, Bobby won a pleasant little one-day medal competition at Suningdale, the London Golf Illustrated Gold Vase tournament, nosing out the Hon. W. G. Brownlow with cards of 75-68—143 against the Hon. Brownlow's 69-75—144. And, in the very last round he played in the British Isles, he really got to hitting the ball in his best mood, and scored a record 66 at Ted Ray's club, Oxhey, in an exhibition match for charity played with his old friends, Harry Vardon, James Braid, and Big Ted. That, I think, was the only round of the trip in which he was satisfied with his performance.

Still, he was carrying two championships home with him. And that is a remarkable illustration of the fact that winning a major golfing competition requires something more than hitting a ball properly—even in the competition itself.

Bobby went out to Minneapolis direct from New York, after another huge welcome, where his mother and father joined him, and Chick

Ridley, an old friend from Atlanta, who accompanied him to the national open championship, while Mary went on home to the children with the rest of the Atlanta party who had gone to Europe. Reaching the scene of the championship, the Interlachen Country Club, Bobby was charmed to find his game apparently working well; certainly better than in either of the big tournaments in Britain. He got in plenty of practice, and started the show with a card of 71, a stroke better than par.

It was one of the hottest days I can remember; the steamy, Turkish-bath sort of heat that rises from pretty little lakes set artistically about the countryside. The thermometer on the shady side of the club registered 101. Bobby did the first nine in 34 and the last nine in an hour and a half and an increasing desire to get under a cool shower. Still, his rather shabby 37 gave him the 71, and that headed the board until late in the afternoon, when Macdonald Smith and Tommy Armour came in with a beautiful 70 each and were tied for the first day's lead.

Bobby's round was finished at the hottest part of the day, and he was so drenched with perspiration that he couldn't unknot his tie and I had to cut it off him so he could get under that shower

in a hurry. Chick Ridley and Colonel Charlie
Cox, of Atlanta, walked with him all the way
around and carried thermos bottles of ice-water,
which is supposed to be a very bad thing to drink
when you are hot and bothered and exercising.
I am doubtful about this, now. Bobby drank
plenty of it and seemed to thrive.

The heat was too much for some of the contestants. Charlie Hall, the hard-hitting professional
from Birmingham—where it occasionally is warm
—brought in a card of 92 in the first round and
gave up.

"This championship," said Charlie, "will go to
the man with the thickest skull!"

After it was all over, on Saturday, I told Bobby
what Charlie had said. He grinned.

"Maybe it did, at that," he rejoined.

Added to the warmth of the weather, Bobby
also was in the hottest kind of a hot spot, in the
championship. At the end of the first round Mac
Smith and Tommy Armour were leading with
70. Bobby was next, tied with Wiffy Cox, at 71.
Walter Hagen, Horton Smith, and Harry Cooper
were tied with 72, which was par. Joe Turnesa
and Craig Wood, at 73; Johnny Farrell, Charles
Lacey, and Johnny Goodman, the little amateur
who had stopped Bobby at Pebble Beach, sharing

READING LEFT TO RIGHT—EDWARD RAY, BOBBY JONES, JAMES
BRAID, HARRY VARDON

(*P. & A. Photos*)

THE LAST STROKE OF THE LAST NATIONAL OPEN CHAMPION-
SHIP—INTERLACHEN, 1930

74, and half a dozen other contenders were very
much in the chase. It isn't so tough, when only
one or two are up their with you. One man, or
even two, may skid a bit. But you can't count on
a whole dozen skidding. Some of them are going
to hang on.

It was next day, after the second round, that I
wrote for my paper a story in which I said that
the gang had Bobby "on the spot"—they were
going to take him for a ride, if they could. It
looked that way. With another ragged last nine,
and a 6 at the fifteenth, Bobby brought in a 73 for
Friday, and his halfway total was 144, exactly
par. This was good enough to shove Mac Smith
and Tommy Armour and Wiffy Cox behind him.
But Horton Smith with a brilliant 70 had gone
into the lead, and Lacey and Cooper, maintaining
a steady pace, moved up to a tie with Bobby.
Bobby was in the thick of a cluster of ten competitors, every one of whom had a chance.

As they started the third round Saturday
morning, the standing of the ten leaders was:

```
Horton Smith ............ 72—70—142
Cooper .................. 72—72—144
Lacey ................... 74—70—144
Jones ................... 71—73—144
Mac Smith ............... 70—75—145
```

Armour	....	70—76—146
Cox	....	71—75—146
Farrell	....	74—72—146
Hagen	....	72—75—147
Golden	....	74—73—147

Not one of these ten was out of the running. Horton Smith, Lacey, and Farrell—the last named after a terrible start—had been improving. Cooper was playing the steadiest golf of the field; each of his two rounds had been 36-36. One bad hole had put Hagen back. It looked as if Bobby was on the spot. He might get two, or four—or six or eight—of these grim musketeers. But I had a cold premonition that one of them, in the end, would get him. The gang had him out for a ride.

And as long as it was to be a ride, Bobby seems to have decided it might as well be a fast one. And Saturday morning he broke away for a 68— a new course record, the lowest round Bobby ever shot in the national open, and, if he could just hang on, the winning margin of the 1930 championship.

There was more than a little good fortune in Bobby's second round, which kept him up in a position to turn on the heat in the third. There was one break, at the ninth hole of the second round, that may very well have meant the championship.

The ninth at Interlachen is a dog-leg to the right, of 485 yards, the second shot a big one across a pretty little lake, to a small, well guarded green. Bobby had been reaching the green, or its vicinity, with a drive and spoon, and in the first round he did a birdie 4 there. His drive in the second round was cut slightly, going a bit off line to the right, and winding up with the ball in a very tight lie near the bank of the lake. It was a hard spoon shot, and Bobby half-topped the ball, which started away at a nearly flat trajectory, certain not to reach the farther bank.

A ball in the water here would cause Bobby to play another from the same bank, plus a penalty stroke. The best he could hope for, in that case, would be a 6—very possibly a 7, if the next effort failed to be on the small green.

It is not too fanciful to say that the fate of a championship was riding on that ball as it struck the water twenty yards from the farther bank, skipped like a flat stone once and again, and hopped out on the smooth slope, thirty yards short of the green.

Accompanied by some thousands of semi-hysterical spectators, Bobby walked slowly around the lake, recovering equilibrium the while, and took full advantage of this gift of the gods by sticking a wee pitch two feet from the flag and holing a birdie 4. That break saved him at least two strokes. He won the championship by two strokes. Nobody can say surely that they were those strokes—or that they were not.

At any rate, there it was. And Bobby was in a tie for second place at the end of the day. And, starting early Saturday morning in the third round, he turned on the heat.

The early start didn't hurt Bobby's performance any, or help his nearest rivals. He finished the first nine with a 33, just as Horton Smith left the first tee. Horton, of course, knew what Bobby had done on the first nine, and from the other side of the course, as Bobby continued his terrific lacing of Old Man Par, came blasts of cheering from a huge gallery ecstatically convinced that history was in the making before its eyes.

And in the face of all that, Horton did nine consecutive 4's on the first nine, and despite Bobby's rush was only a stroke behind at the turn.

Bobby maintained the tremendous pace, the fastest ever set in our open championship, for

the first seven holes coming in. At the seventeenth
tee he needed a par 3 and a par 4 to finish with
a 66. But the strain was getting him. His drive
for the seventeenth, a one-shotter of 262 yards—
the longest par-3 hole I ever saw—was bunkered
short of the green and a 4 was the best he could
do. At the last hole he aimed his drive to the right
of the fairway to keep the line of his second shot
away from a big tree near the left front corner of
the green, and the ball wheeled off into the rough
beside a small tree. He had to pitch out short, and
his third was just over the back of the green. He
chipped close and holed a 5, completing the best
round he ever did in the American open. This was
the card:

```
Par (out) ........ 443  534  445—36
Jones ........... 443  433  345—33

Par (in) ........ 455  344  434—36—72
Jones ........... 444  344  345—35—68
```

Horton Smith could not maintain his par pace
of the first nine holes, slipped to a 40 coming in,
and Harry Cooper went into second place, with
Bobby leading the field by five strokes. The ride
had been too fast for the gang. It was now all
over but holding on.

And, as at Hoylake not long before, Macdon-

ald Smith chased Bobby almost to the wire, starting seven strokes behind him and an hour later.

Bobby began the last round by losing three
strokes to par in the first three holes, and four
strokes to Mac Smith, who started 4-4-2 against
Bobby's 4-5-5. Here was a final chance for a
fatal break. One more bad hole, after that
wretched 5 on the short third, and Bobby might
very well be ruined. But the fourth hole was
good to him, all through the tournament, and
it did not fail him now. Of 506 yards, it was
rated a tough par 5. But every round Bobby did a
4 on it. And here, when he needed it most desperately, he nearly reached the green with two huge
wood shots, pitched close, and holed another 4.
At the turn he had used 38 strokes. Mac Smith,
playing like a man in a trance, was out in 34.
Three strokes behind. Bobby picked up a stroke
at the long eleventh and Mac took it back at the
twelfth, and then got two more back when Bobby,
who was having a ghastly time with the par-3
holes, took a 5 at the 192-yard thirteenth.

At this point, an hour later, Mac Smith was
a single stroke behind. He had gained six strokes
on Bobby, in thirteen holes.

I think, after all, that it was the D'Artagnan in
Bobby who finished that round—who rammed

down a long putt for a birdie 3 at the next hole
after that wretched 5; who picked up another
birdie 3 at the sixteenth; and sliced a wild drive
off the face of the earth into a parallel water hazard at the seventeenth, for another 5; and, at the
finish, sent a 40-foot putt into the hole for a birdie
3 at the seventy-second green; the last stroke of
the championship.

It was that long putt barred the door at Interlachen. An hour later, Mac Smith stood on the
eighteenth tee, a single stroke behind Bobby.
Without that great putt, Mac would have had a
3 to tie. With that putt in the can, it was an impossible 2. He finished with a par 4, and a round
of 70. He had cut away five strokes of a seven-
stroke lead. But Bobby had won. His score was
287, a stroke behind the record for the American
open, made by Chick Evans in 1916 at another
Minneapolis course, Minikahda. Horton Smith
was third, three strokes back of Macdonald Smith.
Cooper and Golden were next.

And Merion—well, that was the last stop.
Bobby came to this decision in an upper room at
the Interlachen club, after his last round. He had
had enough. No matter what happened at Merion,
he was through with competitive golf.

It seems a bit like the pleasant story-books of

our childhood, that Bobby should have finished his
golfing career at the old Merion Cricket Club,
where he started in the Big Show fourteen years
—just half his lifetime—before. It was there, too,
he won his first national amateur championship.
Merion had been the start; it was to be the finish.
And this time, across the familiar fairways of
Merion, stood the last wall of the Impregnable
Quadrilateral, which, to the season of 1930, and
until Bobby Jones came to Merion at the end of
that season, had been regarded only as the rosy
dream of an impossible conquest.

"Last Stop—Merion" said the headlines.

Bobby played badly in practice; his game was
worrying him a lot—but something else was
worrying him more, whether he knew it or not.
He kept right on with the practice rounds until
the last afternoon before the tournament started;
something he never liked to do, if his game was
at all satisfactory. It was that last afternoon he
finally came in with a 69, which he said was decent; and then he felt better. He went very well
in the first qualifying round, with another 69,
and led the field by a stroke. Next day, in the second round, he was playing nearly as consistently,
and when he reached the seventeenth tee he needed
a par 3 and a par 4 for a 71 and a new record for

THREE SIDES OF THE "IMPREGNABLE QUADRILATERAL"—
O. B. KEELER AND BOBBY JONES

AND THE FOURTH

the qualifying round, then held jointly by himself and Ducky Corkran, at 142. A long wait at the seventeenth tee, where several pairs of players and a gallery of eight thousand were backed up, cost him a lot of concentration. He pulled his drive to a bunker and took a 4. At the last hole, being just a trifle annoyed, I fancy, he walloped a tee-shot well over 300 yards, down into a valley in the fairway in front of the green; played a spade-mashie second on a hole of 455-yards, from a spot to which he never had driven before, and the ball went over the green. So he finished with a 5, a card of 73, and a total of 142—tieing the record, and winning the medal, with George Von Elm next, at 143.

On the board, Bobby's matches in his last championship looked easy enough. In the 18-hole bouts he defeated Ross Somerville 5-4 and F. G. Hoblitzel by the same margin. And in the third match, the first of the 36-hole engagements, he showed that he was feeling a sort of strain that never had touched him before. He was missing shots in an unaccountable fashion, against Fay Coleman, and while Coleman was not playing well, Bobby was only 2 up at the intermission.

I went back to his locker with Mickey Cochrane, catcher for the Philadelphia Athletics. Mickey shook hands with Bobby and asked him how he was feeling.

"Fine," was the answer. "I never felt better. But I can't get the shots going right. I don't know what's the matter."

I told Bobby I knew. He asked me to tell him. But I said it wouldn't do any good—he'd just have to work it out for himself, the way he always had worked things out.

After we had walked away Mickey said to me:

"I know what's the matter, too. It's that fourth championship. He's got three in the bag, and the strain is bearing down. It's that way in baseball. When you have a series you simply *have* to win, and you've got it, all but the last game, you'll go out there feeling all right in every way, and everything seems to go all wrong. The old strain is bearing down."

Whether or not Bobby realized what was the matter, he managed to get the shots working better in the afternoon and beat Coleman 6-5. And that put him in the semi-final round with Jess Sweetser, who, in that same round of the amateur champion of 1922 at Brookline, had given him the worst drubbing of his major tournament career.

This match was a very good example of the
way the cumulative strain of the "fourth championship" was affecting Bobby. He started with
a brilliant 3 at the first hole, and won the third,
fourth, and fifth, there being 4 up. He then fired
a shot out of bounds at the seventh, took three
putts at the ninth and tenth greens, and was only
1 up. . . . All week his play was spotty; good
and even brilliant at times; then unsteady—unaccountably unsteady, if you didn't consider that
fourth championship and all that depended on it.

After Jess had hauled him back to 1 up, Bobby
got going again, was 4 up at noon, and, at the
tenth hole of the afternoon round, ended the
match by sticking a short pitch against the pin
for a birdie 3. The margin was 9-8.

After the match Jess came over to Bobby's
locker.

"I did want to carry you to the eleventh green,"
he said, with a grin. "That would have made it
8-7, the same as at Brookline. And then I could
have said, 'Well, Bobby, we're all square, after
eight years.' But I couldn't make it. You're 1
up!"

And I thought of that dismal afternoon at
Brookline, and the long, long walk back to the

clubhouse from the distant eleventh green, after that other semi-final match. . . . It seemed a very long time ago.

Gene Homans, after being 5 down to Charlie Seaver in the morning round, won the match in the other bracket by shooting sixteen pars, one birdie, and one hole over par, for a card of 70 in the afternoon, and he and Bobby met in the finals next day. That finish undoubtedly took a lot out of Gene. Bobby by this time had his game pretty well under control, and he never gave the younger player much of a chance. The match ended at the eleventh green in the afternoon, 8-7. . . . It made quite a picture as the United States Marines charged on to the green, to keep the crowd, also charging, off the players. The Marines had handled the galleries all week; and they did it well.

But the picture I carried away from that last round of the last match of the last championship, at Merion, is a picture of Big Bob Jones standing on a hillside looking down on the fourth green as the match, attended by a vast gallery, came slowly down the long fairway. Big Bob was worried about the match. He always was worried about any match in which Bobby was playing, until the last putt was in the tin. Bobby had a big lead in this last of all his matches, and the holes were running out.

Still, Big Bob was worried. He was saying nothing; just watching the thousands in the gallery slowly topping the hillcrest a quarter of a mile up the fairway and pouring down the slope. But I saw Big Bob cock an eye at a chap who came up at a trot from across the brook, from the direction of the match. Somebody queried him:

"How's the match now?"

The trotting man slowed to a walk.

"He's 8 up," he replied. "It's in the bag."

Big Bob never said a word. His expression did not change a line. He just looked out across the little stream and the smooth valley, and past the first rushing fringe of the gallery, and back along the fairway to where a stocky figure, tiny in the distance, was coming slowly down. Big Bob was humming softly, under his breath. The tune was barely audible. If he had been singing the words, they would have been:

"There's a long, long trail a-winding into the land of my dreams."

So it was good-by, at Merion, as long ago it had been good-morning there. The chunky schoolboy of 1916 had grown into the calm and poised young man whom the world called the master of golf—"matchless in skill and chivalrous in spirit"—and who was not less truly master of himself as well.

CHRONOLOGY

1902.—Born, March 17, Atlanta, Ga.

1908.—Started playing golf. First saw Stewart Maiden.

1911.—At age of nine, won Junior Championship, Atlanta Athletic Club.

1913.—At age of eleven did a score of 80, old course of Atlanta Athletic Club, East Lake.

1915.—Won first invitation tournament away from home, Roebuck Country Club, Birmingham. Played in first Southern Amateur, qualifying in third place, at East Lake.

1916.—Won first Georgia State Amateur, at Capital City Country Club, Atlanta. At age of fourteen qualified in first National Amateur, Merion Cricket Club, Philadelphia. Won first two matches. Lost to Robert A. Gardner in third round.

1917.—Won Southern Amateur, Roebuck C. C., Birmingham. Qualified in Western Amateur, Midlothian C. C., Chicago. Lost to New Sawyer in first round.

1918.—Red Cross Matches with Perry Adair, Alexa Stirling, and Elaine Rosenthal. War Relief Matches with Professionals at Baltusrol, Englewood, Siwanoy and Garden City.

1919.—Runner-up to James M. Barnes, Southern Open at East Lake. Runner-up to J. Douglas Edgar in Canadian Open at Hamilton. Lost to Nelson M. Whitney in semi-final round, Southern Amateur, at New Orleans. Runner-up to S. Davidson Herron, National Amateur, Oakmont.

1920.—Runner-up to J. Douglas Edgar, Southern Open, at East Lake. Won Southern Amateur at Chattanooga. Medalist in Western Amateur at Memphis, losing to Chick Evans in semi-finals. Played in first National Open, Inverness Club, Toledo, finishing in tie for eighth place, four strokes behind Edward Ray of England, winner. Medalist, National Amateur, Engineers Club, Long Island. Lost to Francis Ouimet in semi-finals.

1921.—Played in first British Amateur at Hoylake, England, losing to Allan Graham in fourth round. Played in first British Open at St. Andrews, withdrawing in third round. Tied for fourth place, Western Open at Cleveland. Tied for fifth place, National Open, Columbia C. C., Washington. Lost to Willie Hunter in third round, National Amateur, St. Louis.

1922.—Won Southern Amateur, East Lake. Tied with John Black for second place, runner-up to Gene Sarazen, in National Open at Skokie C. C., Chicago. Won in singles and foursomes, first Walker Cup International Team Match, National Links of America, Long Island. Lost to Jess Sweetser in semi-finals, National Amateur at Brookline.

1923.—Won National Open at Inwood, after play-off with Bobby Cruickshank. Medalist after play-off with Chick Evans, National Amateur, Flossmoor. Lost to Max Marston in second round.

1924.—Won Georgia-Alabama P. G. A. Open, Atlanta. Second in National Open, Oakland Hills, won by Cyril Walker, Won in singles, lost in foursomes, Walker Cup Match, Garden City. Won National Amateur, at Merion.

1925.—Second in National Open after play-off with Willie Macfarlane, at Worcester. Won National Amateur, Oakmont. Tied for third place, Hialeah Open, Miami.

1926.—Defeated in 72-hole match in Florida by Walter Hagen, 12-11. Second in Florida West Coast Open, Pasadena. Lost to Andrew Jamieson in sixth round, British Amateur at Muirfield. Won in singles and foursomes, Walker Cup Match at St. Andrews. Led Southern Section, qualifying for British Open, at Sunningdale, England, with scores of 66-68. Won British Open, Lytham and St. Anne's. Won United States Open, Scioto C. C., Columbus. Medalist, National Amateur at Baltusrol. Lost to George Von Elm in final round.

1927.—Won Southern Open, East Lake. Tied for eleventh place, National Open, at Oakmont. Won British Open at St. Andrews with new record score, 285. Medalist and winner, United States Amateur, Minikahda.

1928.—Second in National Open at Olympia Fields, after play-off with Johnny Farrell. Won in singles and foursomes, Walker Cup Match at Chicago. Captain of American side. Won National Amateur at Brae Burn.

1929.—Won National Open at Winged Foot, in play-off with Al Espinosa. Co-medalist with Gene Homans, National Amateur at Pebble Beach. Lost in first round to John Goodman.

1930.—Runner-up to Horton Smith in Savannah Open.

Won Southeastern Open, Augusta. Won in singles and foursomes, Walker Cup Match at Sandwich, England. Captain of American side. Won London Golf Illustrated Gold Vase at Sunningdale. Won British Amateur at St. Andrews. Won British Open at Hoylake. Won United States Open at Interlachen. Won United States Amateur at Merion. Retired from competitive golf.

MAJOR CHAMPIONSHIPS

United States Amateur, 1924, 1925, 1927, 1928, 1930.
United States Open, 1923, 1926, 1929, 1930.
British Open, 1926, 1927, 1930.
British Amateur, 1930.